PROBLEMS IN EXPOSITION
FOR THE PRACTICAL STYLIST

PROBLEMS IN EXPOSITION
FOR THE
PRACTICAL STYLIST

SHERIDAN BAKER
DWIGHT STEVENSON

Both of The University of Michigan

THOMAS Y. CROWELL COMPANY
New York   Established 1834

PROBLEMS IN EXPOSITION FOR THE PRACTICAL STYLIST

ISBN 0-690-00875-9

77 78 79 80 7 6 5 4 3 2

Preface

You learn by writing. You learn to write well by rewriting, by trying repeatedly to get your thoughts down on paper clearly, and across to the reader attractively. The exercises in PROBLEMS IN EXPOSITION will sharpen and help you control skills learned in THE PRACTICAL STYLIST by doing, and redoing, more of the same in numerous ways. These practices follow THE PRACTICAL STYLIST, Fourth Edition, taking you step by step through the problems of writing an essay—finding a thesis and focusing the essay; then shaping a great variety of paragraphs, tuning sentences, and choosing words. You will also remove the rust from your writing mechanics with the added practice in grammar, punctuation, spelling, and capitalization. For longer compositions, practice in outlining and documentation complete the basic machinery.

The exercises emphasize the value of economy, and the fun of trying to beat the word-score of our standard clumsy prose. Many examples in the text and exercises come from both professional bungles and classroom tangles. And you are invited to revise some of your own attempts as well, just as we had to do quite often in composing PROBLEMS IN EXPOSITION.

Write on these pages and tear them out for your instructor's marking. You can work most of the exercises directly on the pages in this book; for some of the larger exercises, such as paragraphs and outlines, you will need extra sheets. Though they can stand alone, the exercises in PROBLEMS IN EXPOSITION deliver the greatest benefits when worked with the exercises in THE PRACTICAL STYLIST. Preceding each main topic in PROBLEMS is a cross-reference to the matching discussion in THE PRACTICAL STYLIST.

This book can be diagnostic as well as curative. Your instructor may prefer to employ these exercises to ascertain where you need extra practice, whether in paragraphing, or constructing sentences, or handling punctuation and mechanics. Or your instructor may take another tack and let the exercises in this book amplify those in THE PRACTICAL STYLIST. Diagnosis or cure, PROBLEMS IN EXPOSITION can, in many ways, conquer your own writing problems.

The publisher, on request, will furnish instructors using PROBLEMS IN EXPOSITION with our suggested solutions to the exercises.

S.B.
D.S.

Contents

1 Thesis and Structure

The central idea, or thesis, of your essay is its life and spirit. If you have a limited, energetic, and—above all—clear central assertion, your essay will go a long way toward writing itself. You have taken a stand. Perhaps your thesis even indicates *why* you've taken that stand. All that remains is for you to convince your reader that your stand is the only sensible one. In short, before you begin writing, make sure you have a clear thesis. As shown in *The Practical Stylist (TPS)* a subject will tell you only vaguely what your essay is "on." A thesis, on the other hand, will tell you what you are going to *do* with the subject.

But trying to develop a good essay from a *poorly stated* thesis is like trying to swim in a suit of armor: you can go through the motions; you can thrash around and kick, but—chances are—you will still end up sinking. In short, you need to spot the trouble *before* you begin to write; you need to develop the habit of looking for *potential trouble* in your thesis statements.

Exercise 1: Sharpening the Thesis

The following sentences are thesis statements taken from students' papers. Explain what, if anything, you think wrong with each of these as thesis statements. Then, using the guidelines in *The Practical Stylist*, revise them as best you can.

1. The campus of —— University (College) is unique in many ways.

____

____

2. With the increasing enrollment at this university (and with the larger number of married students) steps need to be taken to increase student housing.

____

____

____

3. From experience, I would believe that weight-lifting can be helpful to a growing young man in more ways than one.

____

____

____

4. The two-mile, cross-country run is one of the most challenging of track events. It requires speed, endurance, and strategy.

____

____

____

5. No matter how it used to be in this country, we have an aristocracy of money now.

____

____

____

6. Joseph Heller's *Catch-22* is not great literature. Indeed, the book is not really a novel at all; it is just a series of little stories.

____

____

____

____

____

7. I believe, and will try to show, that the unequal distribution of blacks and whites in occupational groups revealed in the last Census is the result of two problems: inferior education for blacks and discriminatory hiring by white employers.

____

____

____

____

____

____

8. Could half-day sessions in elementary schools provide the same quality of education as provided by full-day sessions?

____

____

____

9. The tourist trade only brings financial gain for a specialized and limited segment of the population.

____

____

____

10. Hunting rules should be changed so that novices could get only small-game permits.

____

____

11. Lake Michigan, one of the most beautiful bodies of water in the world, is rapidly losing much of its appeal.

____

____

____

12. The majority of the spectators at a boxing match are there to see pain, blood, and agony.

____

____

____

13. It is believed that Hawthorne's short prose narratives influenced Melville in writing *The Piazza Tales*.

____

____

____

14. Senator Edwards will be sorry he surfaced as a candidate long before he was ready.

____

____

____

15. Automation does not reduce the number of available jobs.

____

____

Acknowledging the Opposition   *TPS*, pp. 10–14

Any controversial topic demands handling not only one's own argument, but the opposition's argument as well. Otherwise, you are a shadowboxer whose only opposition is a pretense that can't punch back. The fancy footwork, the showy jabs, the roundhouse punch mean nothing unless two flesh-and-blood fighters are in the ring.

Anticipating your opponent's arguments gives you an obvious tactical advantage. Like the fighter who gets his feet set and his guard up, you know what is coming and you are ready for it. So, as you write, admit to yourself that there *is* a worthy opposition, that you aren't just shadowboxing. Recognize your opposition's arguments, and prepare for them.

An *organizational principle* reinforces this tactical one. You don't, of course, want to give your opposition the last word. You don't want to save all *his* arguments for the end of *your* paper, and finish by apparently making his case for him. Instead, you want to start by getting his arguments out of the way, and finish by establishing your own position. If your opposition is lightweight, a paragraph or two at the beginning of the essay should serve to dispose of him. If, on the other hand, your opposition has a number of points to make, you will probably want to meet his points one at a time. For both cases, the principle is the same: put your opposition's arguments first, and demolish them before going on to your own arguments. The organization of a simple argument might look like this:

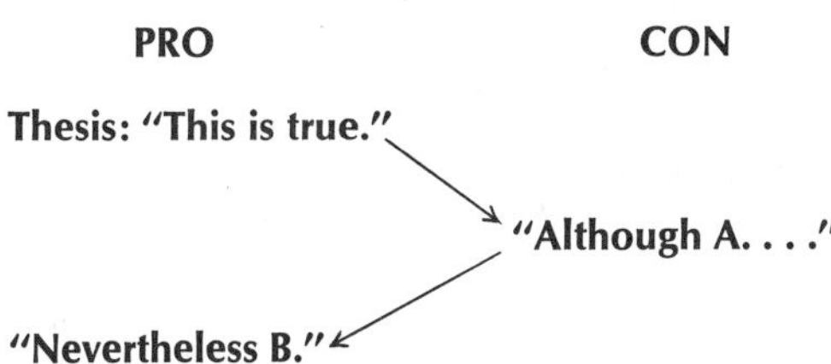

On the other hand, a more complex argument might be organized like this:

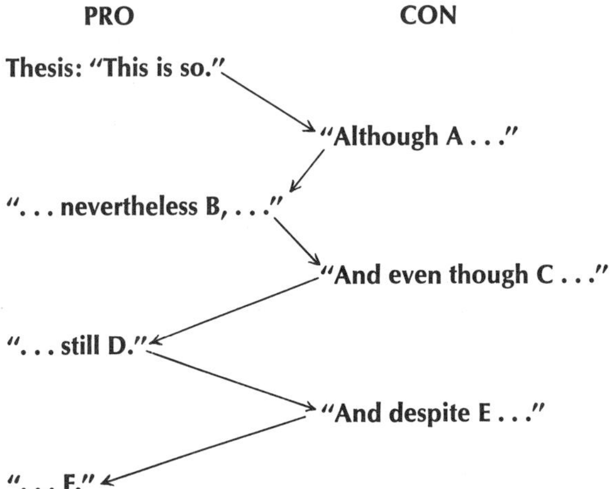

Exercise 2: Acknowledging the Opposition

A series of general assertions follows. Supply one argument *against* **and one argument** *for* **each proposition. Then combine the statements into one thesis sentence that includes not only the assertion but also the reasons against and for it.**

0. (Example Exercise) Assertion: Movies should not be censored.
   Con: Children should not be exposed to obscene and explicitly sexual images on the screen.
   Pro: Obscenity is far too subjective a thing for any person to define for anyone else.
   Thesis Statement: Although it is probably undesirable for young people to be exposed to scenes of explicit sex in films, movies still should not be censored because obscenity is so subjective a thing that no one can legitimately serve as censor for the rest of us.

1. Assertion: Discussion classes are superior to lectures.
2. Assertion: Rapid and convenient transit systems must be built in our cities.
3. Assertion: The federal government should subsidize large companies forced near bankruptcy by cuts in defense spending.
4. Assertion: Medical schools should reduce the time required for a degree in general medicine from four years to two.
5. Assertion: States should prohibit the sale of beverages in nonreturnable containers.
6. Assertion: A guaranteed annual income would not wipe out poverty for all Americans.
7. Assertion: As exercise, golf is a waste of time.
8. Assertion: Rear-engine cars are dangerous.
9. Assertion: College students should study a foreign language.
10. Assertion: Smoking should be outlawed in all places, such as restaurants, theaters, offices, factories, where the public gathers outside the home.

Comparing Point by Point   *TPS*, pp. 10–14

The preceding exercise focused upon comparatively short and uncomplicated examples of controversy in which we pretended that the opposition had only one major
argument and that you claim only one major argument yourself. For example: "There
should be no censorship of movies because [your opposition] although young people
should probably not be exposed to explicit sex in films, [your own argument]
obscenity is so subjective a thing that no one can legitimately serve as censor for the
rest of us." Of course, in most genuine controversies your opposition will come up
with a half-dozen arguments against your thesis, and—if you hope to convince
anybody but yourself—you will come up with at least as many in your defense. In
short, most real controversy is give-and-take, summing up, and adding and subtracting
the consequences of a number of arguments; it is not often the head-to-head collision
of one simple assertion with another. Yet, even in the most complicated of arguments,
the tactical and organizational principles we examined in the last exercise still apply.
Meet and dispose of your opposition point by point. And arrange your argument so
that you move from the lesser to the greater of your proofs, finishing with your best
ammunition.

Exercise 3: Comparing Point by Point

In the exercise that follows, you will find an essay in which the author advances his
thesis point by point. On a separate sheet, state the thesis, then number and identify
the arguments both for and against the thesis. Also identify as *con* or *pro* the words
or phrases the author uses to mark the switch from one side of the argument to the
other. In the essay itself, underline and number the arguments for and against the
assertion, circle the transitional devices, and draw in arrows that indicate whether the
author is rejecting the opposition or advancing his own assertion.

I should start by admitting that as little as five years ago carpeted class-

rooms would rightly have been regarded as a fanciful and expensive luxury.

The carpeting then available would have been costly, difficult to maintain,

and would have required frequent replacement. Now, however, because of

improved materials, the arguments in favor of extensive use of carpeting seem

a great deal more plausible. New indoor-outdoor synthetics—stain resistant,

fade resistant, durable, and inexpensive—have made carpeting seem much

less a luxury than a reasonable, even desirable, alternative to tile floors.

Briefly, there seem to be three central arguments in favor of the extensive use

of carpeting.

First, of course, carpeting is clearly desirable for aesthetic reasons. Now, admittedly, there is a great variety of attractively colored tiles available, and the days of the drab, institutional grays, greens, and browns in tile are—happily—over. But, even though tile may approach carpeting in terms of color, it still has a hard and unattractive texture. Carpeting, on the other hand, is colorful, attractive to touch, and comfortable to walk on. It goes a long way toward creating a pleasant atmosphere all of us would like to work in, both in and out of class. Richly colored carpeting, such as the bold reds often used in banks, restaurants, department stores, and commercial offices, would make our facilities far less "institutional." Bright carpeting can easily make attractive an area that would otherwise seem Spartan and sterile. In short, carpeting seems desirable simply because it is more attractive to look at and walk on than tile.

The second argument in favor of carpeted classrooms is essentially pragmatic: carpeting serves a useful acoustical function. It is true, of course, that the flexible backing and roughened texture of new tiles available on the market make them far less noisy than tiles available just a few years ago. Just as there have been advances in the carpeting industry, there have also been significant advances in the tile industry. Carpeting, however, is an excellent sound dampener; it cuts noise from crowded hallways, absorbs annoying background noise in classrooms—scuffing feet, scooting chairs, coughs—and makes busy space less noisy and, therefore, much more practical. In industry, if not in schools, one frequently finds carpeting being used because it makes heavily used areas more functional by reducing noise.

A final argument in favor of extensive use of carpeting is that, over a period of time, carpeting appears to be no more expensive than floor tile. Certainly it is true that the cost of carpeting is initially much higher than the cost of tile, and it does need eventual replacement. So, if one calculates only the initial cost, tile is admittedly cheaper than carpeting. On the other hand, the cost of maintaining carpeting is minimal when compared to the cost of maintaining tile floors, which need frequent washing, waxing, and dusting. The new synthetic carpet materials are resistant to stains and fading, and all that one needs to maintain them is an ordinary household vacuum cleaner. The tile floor, unfortunately, needs frequent scrubbing and waxing if it is not to look dull and yellow with accumulated wax. And not only is this a laboriously slow process, but also, in large institutions, it is impossible to do without large and expensive scrubbing machines. In short, if one computes the cost of tile and carpeting only in their initial investment, tile is clearly cheaper. If, on the other hand, one computes the cost overall, the differences between the two disappear and carpeting becomes a legitimate economic alternative to tile.

Were it not for the obvious advantages in appearance and acoustics of carpeting over tile, one could perhaps argue fairly in favor of conventional flooring. After all, the cost differences figured over a very long period, say 20 or 30 years, are genuinely unpredictable. We simply haven't yet accumulated enough experience with the new synthetics, and perhaps it will turn out in the end that the cost of carpeting figured over a quarter of a century is a good deal higher. Perhaps we will discover that, after a decade or so, the cost advantages of carpeting evaporate. To this point, however, our experience with synthetic materials is essentially affirmative. And so, given the clear edge carpeting has over tile aesthetically and acoustically, and given its apparent economic justification, carpeting for classrooms seems completely sensible.

Dialectics   *TPS*, pp. 10–14

Perhaps the term *dialectics* **is unfamiliar to you. If so, don't let that bother you, because in the preceding two exercises we have already seen the essential dialectic principles: acknowledgment of an opposition and dealing with it first.**

Briefly, dialectics is the logical discussion employed to discover truth. It is the

weighing and reconciling of contradictory opinions. It is debate. The essential notion is dialogue, give-and-take, a question-and-answer meeting of an assertion with its opposition.

As the writer you are obviously partisan: you are trying to defend one side against another. But ignoring your opponent makes little sense. On the one hand, you will never prove your point by concealing arguments against it. On the other hand, you may well strengthen your argument by finding out what is good in your opposition's defense. After all, you cannot reasonably suppose that he has nothing valid to say. So take him seriously, treat his arguments fairly, and learn from them. Then build the best defense you know.

Exercise 4: Dialectics

In this exercise, you will find the complete text of two speeches in the House of Representatives. The Honorable William M. Colmer and The Honorable John W. McCormack were voicing their opinions on a constitutional amendment proposing the direct election of the President. McCormack defends; Colmer attacks. After you have read each of the speeches carefully, write an essay supporting either Representative McCormack or Representative Colmer. Employ dialectics: swing the argument back and forth from *pro* to *con* with such transitional words as *to be sure, however, some may think, I concede that.* Make sure you always begin with your opposition and end with your own side. The structural line of your paper might look something like this:

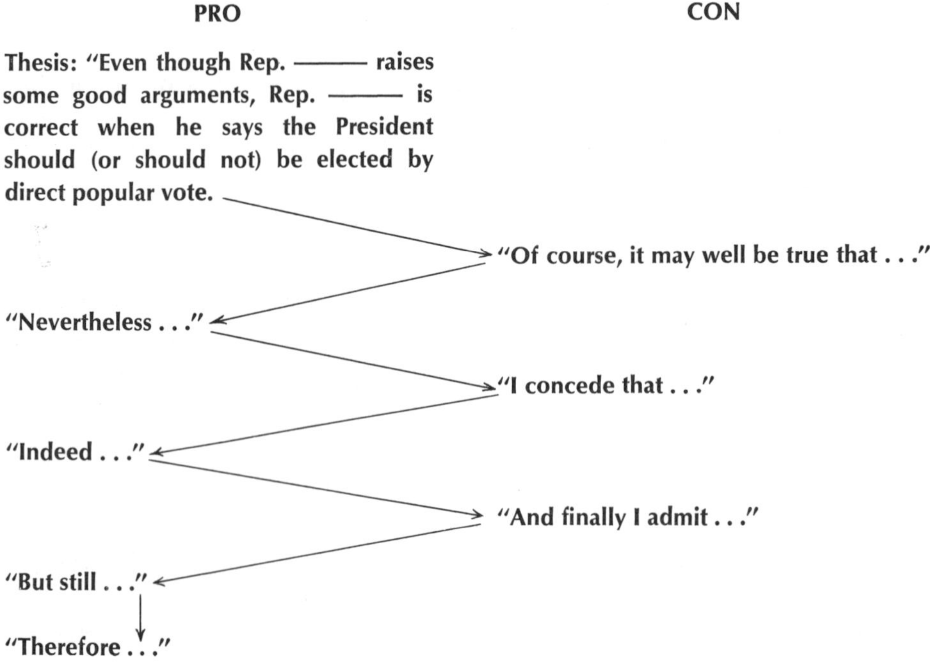

by Hon. John W. McCormack
Speaker of the House of Representatives
September 15, 1969, from the floor of the U.S. House of Representatives

Almost everyone, both in and out of Congress, admits that reform of our electoral college system is long overdue. The present procedure, which permits any elector to switch his vote and frustrate the wishes of the electorate, should be corrected. With luck, we have, so far, escaped a situation in which the defection of electors in violation of their moral obligation has significantly affected the results of our election. We should not and cannot afford to tempt fate further. It is also imperative that we revise the constitutional provisions applicable to deadlocks. The provision that in a deadlock the House should elect the President with one vote cast by each State delegation, as it did on two occasions in the past, certainly could prove harmful in the future.

It is possible, for example, that if a congressional delegation should split evenly, the population of an entire State would lose all voice in choosing a President. It is also possible that a candidate who decisively trailed in the popular vote could be elected President. Also under the present system the other body could elect as Vice President a candidate from a party different from that of the President-elect. Thus the present second election procedures are plainly archaic and, in fact, could be dangerous as the House stands today at the threshold of reforming its electoral process. We must bear in mind that the Office of President of the United States is the most powerful Office in the world. The process by which our people elect the Chief Executive must be attuned to the needs of not only today but tomorrow, and not of decades gone by.

The electorate no longer needs a group of intermediaries known as electors to register their choice. Direct election of the President, it must be acknowledged, is the only method by which the democratic principle of one man, one vote can be effectuated.

The proposed amendment also would conform the contingent election procedures to those of the initial election. The people would elect the President under all circumstances. Only the direct popular election will assure, in the first instance and in a contingency, that the candidate with the greatest popular vote would become President. The direct popular election method which the House is called upon to approve will substitute clarity for confusion and decisiveness for danger, and assure that the popular choice, rather than political chance, will determine the winner and will obviate any future constitutional crisis.

We all know what the history of presidential elections in our country is. For example, in the 46 presidential elections, under the electoral college system, three candidates who received less than a plurality of the popular vote were elected President: Adams in 1824, Hayes in 1876, and Harrison in 1888. Two Presidents were elected by the House: Jefferson in 1800 and Adams in 1824. We know what happened in 1876 in the case of the Hayes election and the Special Electoral Commission appointed by the Congress.

Each one of those cases had the potential of constitutional instability. If it were not for the bigness of the men who had received the popular vote but who were not elected President, there could have been a constitutional crisis in any one of those elections.

The emotionalism that existed could have divided our country. They were big men who assumed the responsibility of unity within our country rather than take the pathway that might have led to emotionalism and disunity.

I recognize the sincerity of those who favor the other plans. I might say in all frankness any one of the two substantial ones are better than the present system, but in my opinion the resolution reported out by the Committee on the Judiciary is the best assurance that we can have that we are giving to the country in the future the maximum of constitutional stability. It seems to me on the basic ground of constitutional stability, and making every contribution we can to assure it in the future, the resolution reported by the Committee commands the respect, the attention, the support, and the vote of at least two-thirds of the Members of this House. So with all respect to the other methods, I urge that they not be adopted and that the resolution reported by the Committee pass this body. It is one means that will give to the maximum extent possible assurances to the people of America and the people of tomorrow that there will be constitutional stability, and that is a matter of vital importance.*

The Congressional Digest, 49 (1970), p. 10.

by Hon. William M. Colmer
United States Representative, Mississippi, Democrat
September 16, 1969, from the floor of the U.S. House of Representatives

We often hear it said that this issue, whatever it may be, is the most important issue that will come before this Congress. I do not think there is any question about it.

For over 170 years or so—and I have not checked on it—this system we have heard criticized here for the past several days has functioned pretty well. There were a couple of times when it failed to elect a President on the first ballot. Under that system we have enjoyed the greatest degree of freedom that any people have enjoyed. This country has prospered as no other country in the history of the world has prospered.

Now do not misunderstand me. I do not say that there is not room for reform. There is. I think that this Congress should adopt the necessary reform. But I cannot agree—I cannot bring myself to agree—with the majority of the Committee on the Judiciary who reported this bill.

Sure there is room for reform. Incidentally, this may not be politically wise to say it—but I am going to say what everyone of you know to be the truth—if it had not been for a man down in Alabama seeking the Presidency, we would not be debating this bill today.

Now I am not holding any brief for the candidate from Alabama. I am just making a statement of fact. You know, we have a way here in this Congress, and I have seen it over the past 37 years—that something happens—we get a few letters from home, and then we get into a spirit of hysteria and we legislate under a condition of emergency.

This is no exception. I repeat. We have done pretty well under the old system. But I am not only willing but ready to go along with some reform, some change. I want to repeat what I said to a few of you here the other day. I do not want to spin my wheels. I do not want to see the Congress spin its wheels merely because someone thinks there is popular appeal in the proposed measure. I admit there is. I admit that to those who have not studied this question the popular appeal is there. So if you are thinking about that aspect of the question, I would have to say I think possibly the thing for you to do is to go ahead and vote for the committee resolution.

But I do not think it is the best bill. As has been pointed out repeatedly here in colloquy, polls are not the most accurate gauge of public opinion, and certainly they are not the criteria of what is the best course for this country to take.

I would accept the proportionate plan, but I think the district plan is the better one.

Maybe I do not believe in radical changes and emergency legislation in amending the Constitution, undoubtedly, the finest document of human liberty ever devised. But if you are going to pursue that method, then why do you not go "whole hog," as they say in my State, and go for the "50 per cent plus one" plan rather than stopping with 40 per cent? You are talking about splinter parties, and that is what you really will create. You are going to have more splinter parties under the Committee's proposal than you have ever had under the old system, because a candidate has to get only 40 per cent plurality in order to be elected President. You are going to find splinter parties coming up in every direction.

I think if this system had been in effect the last election, we would have had many splinter parties. We might have had several of them. We know several gentlemen who were candidates for the Presidency had substantial following.

So if we are going to go this route, then why do we not go all the way and say that in order to be elected the President of the United States, a candidate must receive 50 per cent or more of the vote?

Now there is another angle of this thing that disturbs me. The Founding Fathers, jealous of the rights of the States, said we are going to have a Federal State system where the States will select the electors who will elect the President. We are going to do away with all that now, which is another step in the centralization of the power of Government over the governed in the Federal system. We are going to do away with and abolish the rights of the States.

As to the practicality of the matter, we say we want reform. Everybody seems to be for reform and they want some revision. Whether the

small States have an advantage or not, they think they do. I think they do.
So if we get by now with two-thirds vote in this House—and that is two-
thirds of the Membership, a quorum being present and voting, remember
—then the proposal has to run the gauntlet on the other side of the
Capitol, where there are more than 13 of the so-called smaller States who
think they enjoy some advantage here, and I doubt very seriously if they
will pass the committee resolution. But, assuming they do, then we have to
run the gauntlet of the ratification by three-fourths of the States, and again
these practical politicians in the States are going to be slow to give up
what they regard as an advantage under the present system.

So my plea is if Members want to change the present system, if
Members really want to accomplish something instead of trying to appease
the pollsters and to verify their opinion, then Members had better pass the
district plan, which retains at least a part of the present system and will
not deprive the smaller States of the advantage they enjoy.*

* *The Congressional Digest,* 49 (1970), pp. 11, 13.

2 The Essay: Basic Paragraphs

Middle Paragraphs   *TPS*, pp. 16–19, 20–22

In the middle of things. Perhaps that is a good place for us to start our examination of paragraphs, in the middle. If you think about it in simple quantitative terms, most essays are nearly all middle, with only one paragraph of beginning and one of conclusion. And then too, the opening and closing paragraphs are special-purpose paragraphs, two special pieces of equipment designed for very specific functions, one to get you into an essay, and one to get you out. The good middle paragraph, on the other hand, is a common denominator of all good essays, and if you are able to write a good middle paragraph, you are well on your way to the finished product.

To refresh your memory, let us quickly run over four principles of paragraphing.

First, think of the middle paragraph as a miniature essay, with a beginning, a middle, and an end. Its beginning normally will be your topic sentence, or the thesis of your miniature essay. Its middle will be the development, explanation, or proof of your topic sentence. Its ending will be the reassertion of your topic sentence, the emphatic driving home of your idea. So remember the first principle: your paragraphs should have a beginning, a middle, and an end.

Second, be sure your paragraphs are coherent; that is, everything in the paragraph must be adequately covered by the topic sentence. And you want all your sentences to function together grammatically, stylistically, and intellectually, without any extraneous ideas.

Third, make your paragraphs full and well developed. Too often, beginning writers tend to jump from topic sentence to topic sentence without really bothering to develop the ideas as they go along. The result is always a skeletal paper with very little meat on its bones. So be sure you develop your topic sentence; put in details, examples, and full explanations.

Fourth, remember that although each paragraph is a miniature essay, it is also part of a larger essay. Therefore, be sure to use clear transitions, to hook each paragraph into the paragraphs that precede and follow it. In short, make sure each paragraph has at least some small transitional touch.

Exercise 1: Middle Paragraphs

Select one of the topic sentences from the list given, and develop from it a full middle paragraph in which you consciously try to observe the four principles mentioned above. Remember, the paragraph you write is supposed to be a single paragraph from the middle section of a longer paper; therefore, you will have to imagine what comes before and after the paragraph you write. Here is an example:

> *Topic sentence:* The fashions current in the middle 1970's suggest the same urge we have already seen in films and music to get back to a simpler and more secure past.
>
> The fashions current in middle 1970's suggest the same urge we have already seen in films and music to get back to a simpler and more secure past. For the more stylish dressers among us, the Sunday supplements and fashion magazines are featuring 1920's, 1930's, and 1940's styles in both men's and women's clothing. On the street, you can see fashionable women in broad-shouldered and boxy suits, middy blouses, or "sensible shoes" with ugly, clomping heels, all clearly echoing the past. Or you can see modish men wearing huge bow ties for the first time in thirty years. And you see them wearing the wide lapels, fitted waists, flared trousers, and patterned shirts of the 1920's and 1930's. Even for the anti-Establishment or Bohemian dressers among us, the styles current in the early 1970's reflect the urge to get back to the past. Bibbed overalls, work shirts, clodhoppers, bandannas, wide belts, and Western hats, all conjure up images of a frontier past. Undergraduates go to class dressed like "sod-busters," trappers, or miners fresh from the Virginia City of the 1880's. And in any city park you can find a guitar player whose long hair, beard, and fringed leather jacket would make him appear completely at home in the turn-of-the-century West. It is as if all of us, from the solid Establishment to the Bohemian youth-culture, are seeking by our dress to recapture a more simple and secure past. It is as if we are trying to escape the complexity of the 1970's by costuming ourselves in the styles of the past. We are like children who escape by playing dress-up.

1. But no matter what the advertisements promise, the X-rated movie usually turns out to be dull and wearisome; it turns out to be two hours of heavy breathing.
2. The computer also has contributed to the modern sense of alienation.
3. But if the filibuster is supposed to guarantee respect for minority opinion, it usually turns out to be a flagrant waste of time.

4. Another aspect of the new sense of black pride is our increasing awareness of black accomplishments in the past.
5. But if women are discriminated against in business and in government, they are far more discriminated against in law.

Beginning Paragraphs

TPS, pp. 18–20

The first few moves in a chess game are innocent, slow, and anticipatory. You do not immediately rush into the attack. You set it up carefully, first moving out a pawn, then guarding it with another pawn, and then perhaps moving a knight to its initial position. Only after these opening moves are you ready to begin your attack. The same is true of the opening paragraph of a good paper. You do not immediately jump into your thesis. You take time, four or five or six sentences, to set it up. Only when you are ready, only when you are sure you have the reader's interest, attention, and understanding, do you really move out. Remember, your opening paragraph is the first meeting between you and your reader, and if you bore him, or antagonize him, or—worse still—confuse him, the chances are good that no matter how certain you are of the rest of your paper, you have lost him before he finishes the first paragraph. Don't assume that your reader *has* to read the paper; don't assume that he will be so generous as to read it despite a bad opening. Rather, assume that you have to make him *want* to read the paper.

The paragraph needed to perform this opening function is essentially an inductive paragraph, or, as we call it, the funnel. Its topic sentence, the thesis sentence of the entire essay, comes at the end, not at the beginning of the paragraph. And the opening sentences that lead your reader down to the thesis should be broad and genial, the pleasant first meeting between writer and reader. Open broadly, then narrow down.

Here is an example of an opening paragraph:

The coal operators will tell you that stripping is cheaper and more efficient than conventional mining. Their 250-cubic-yard draglines, their 200-cubic-yard shovels, their 50-ton trucks can rip the top off a mountain and expose a whole seam of coal in a fraction of the time it takes to sink a shaft. "It is cheaper," they will say, "to bring the surface to the coal than to bring the coal to the surface." And of course they are right; in a sense it is cheaper. But visit Eastern Kentucky and look at the real price we pay for stripped coal. Visit a stripped area and you will see that, no matter how low the price for a truckload of stripped coal, the real price for strip-mining has to be reckoned in terms of blighted land, poisoned streams, and stunted human lives.

Exercise 2: Beginning Paragraphs

Below is a list of thesis sentences. Choose one, and incorporate it into the opening paragraph of an essay. Make your funnel-paragraph at least six or seven sentences in length.

1. Since the primary responsibility of business managers is to their stockholders instead of society at large, the federal government, to protect society's interests, must supervise Big Business closely.
2. Camper buses and vans, though they are now regulated, should face the same federal safety requirements as automobiles.
3. "Affirmative action (concentration by business and government on hiring and promoting women and minorities)" has corrected many injustices from the past, but in doing so it has committed many new ones.
4. We may face a repeating cycle of prosperity and recession, but Big Government only slows the natural recovery of a basically healthy economy from a temporary drop.
5. Although many cities and some states have strict gun laws, only the federal government can control the circulation of guns, since uncontrolled possession of guns is a national and not merely a local problem.

End Paragraphs   *TPS*, pp. 22–23

The end paragraph is the beginning paragraph upside-down; it is the structural opposite and complement of the beginning paragraph. Thus, you begin the end paragraph with a restatement of your thesis, often in somewhat altered form. In a longer paper, you will probably want to summarize the points you have made, re-collecting the various parts into a tidy whole. In a short paper, of course, no summary is necessary, and you may move directly from the restatement of your thesis to the pleasant task of leading your reader to see its broader implications. You end the paper as you began it, on a broad and genial note; you move from the particulars back to the general again. Here is an example:

> So, at last, we should add up the *real* costs of strip-mining; we should admit that the ultimate price of coal is far too high if we must rape the land, poison the streams, and wreck human lives to mine it. For after the draglines have gone, even after the coal itself has been burned, the bills for strip-mining will keep coming in. So far, following the expedient path, we have laid bare more than 2,600 square miles of our land, and we show no signs of stopping. Every year we strip an additional 50,000 acres. Just as we cut down our forests in the nineteenth century and fouled our air in the twentieth, we still blunder along toward ecological and social disaster. Isn't it time to stop?

Exercise 3: End Paragraphs

Using the same thesis sentences as in the preceding exercise, write at least two end paragraphs for imaginary papers.

The Whole Essay   *TPS,* pp. 24–26

Beginning, middle, and end: those are the parts. Now let us put them together in a short essay, using the suggestions we have made about paragraphs. Three or four paragraphs will do for a start. Remember, the beginning paragraph should look like a funnel, working from broad opening to a specific statement of your thesis. The middle paragraphs should be miniature essays, each with a topic sentence, development, and end. And finally, your last paragraph should look like an inverted funnel, first restating your thesis, then broadening out to suggest its implications.

An example of a very short essay that incorporates some of the features we have been talking about is "North of the Tracks" in *TPS,* pp. 25–26.

Exercise 4: The Whole Essay

In the two preceding exercises, you have already written the opening and closing portions of an essay. Now, using any of the thesis sentences in Exercise 2, or some similar thesis sentence of your own, develop the whole text of a short essay.

Paragraphs: Some Models

ILLUSTRATION

You will develop a great many of your paragraphs by illustration. You begin with a topic sentence that asserts an idea. Perhaps you follow it with a sentence or two of explanation. And then you peg down your generalization by presenting either a single extended example or a series of short examples. Either way will work well. Finally, you end with a sentence that brings you back to your generalization, reasserting your topic so that the reader does not lose sight of it. From a student's paper, here is a sample paragraph that uses a single, extended example:

But if the Elizabethan playwright had to be anything, he had to be a showman who could entertain and delight his audiences with the kinds of spectacle they loved so well. Witness, for example, Christopher Marlowe, whose play *The Tragical History of Doctor Faustus* was one of the most popular plays ever presented upon the Elizabethan stage. The play begins with the protagonist, Dr. Faustus, acquiring supernatural powers by signing a pact with the devil, Mephistopheles, who first appears before the audience "in the shape of a dragon." From that point on, as Faustus exercises his magical power, the stage is filled with showy and miraculous scenes, one after the other. Elaborately costumed angels, clowns, and devils appear. A Pope, Helen of Troy, an Emperor, and The Seven Deadly Sins, all troop across Marlowe's stage. The ghost of Alexander the Great shows up. There are pantomimes, dances, and songs in quick succession. And the sound effects must be exciting too for fireworks are exploded on stage several times during the play. But, best of all, from the Elizabethan point of view, there is a good lot of violence and vulgar sexual humor sprinkled throughout. Oh, of course, the play ends piously enough: Faustus loses his soul for having bargained with the devil. But for two hours, at least, Marlowe gave Faustus—and his Elizabethan audience—a heady excursion through all the pleasures of this world. The fact that the play was enormously popular and frequently revived on the Elizabethan stage is good evidence that Marlowe knew what his audience wanted and gave it to them.

Exercise 5: Illustration

Write two illustrative paragraphs that might appear in the same essay (not necessarily consecutively). In one, use a single, extended example; in the other, use a series of short examples. For instance, in the preceding excerpt the student would have shortened his example from Marlowe, then added similar examples from Shakespeare, Jonson, Kyd, and so on.

CITATION OF AUTHORITY

Nothing is more deadly than the paper that leaps from assertion to assertion, each defended by appeals to obscure authorities. Madison Avenue has made a business of it, and students often mistake it for scholarship. But a well-cited authority extends your own experience and expertise, backing your own ideas. Here is a sample paragraph from a paper in which a student is discussing the ghetto riots of the summer of 1967:

> But the real cause of the riots seems to go much deeper than that. It has to do with the whole history of white-black relations in this country and is, strictly speaking, neither the consequence of a peculiar set of events in the summer of 1967 nor the result of a freakish and isolated accident. It was not the heat, it was not an incident of police brutality, it was not militant agitation that caused the riots, though all these things perhaps contributed. Rather, it was the long unchanged pattern of attitude and behavior of most white Americans toward black Americans that caused the violent summer of 1967. It was, as the Kerner Commission Report maintains, race prejudice that caused the riots. If the heat, or police, or agitators, provided the spark, nonetheless, as the Commission Report states, "White

racism is essentially responsible for the explosive mixture which has been
accumulating in our cities since the end of World War II."*

* Report of the National Advisory Commission on Civil Disorders (New York:
Bantam Books, Inc., 1969), p. 203.

Exercise 6: Citation of Authority

**Supply a paragraph from your own writing that is developed by citing authority. If
there is none in any of the essays you have already written, write one now that might
appear as part of a full essay.**

COMPARISON

**An occasional comparison or analogy can help your reader grasp an idea by showing
him how it is like something familiar. A paragraph of comparison has a simple pattern
of development: the topic sentence asserts the comparison; the rest of the paragraph
develops the analogy in detail. Two words of caution, however. Analogy works well
only for clarification, not for argument, so you should not assume that by drawing a
comparison you are adding much to the defense of an assertion. And second, analogy
is best when it is simple and brief. Too long a run is tiresome. Here are two examples
from Mark Twain's** *Life on the Mississippi.* **In the first, Twain explains at some length
the riverboat pilot's feat of memory. In the second, he makes the same point again,
more briefly.**

But I am wandering from what I was intending to do, that is, make
plainer than perhaps appears in the previous chapters some of the peculiar
requirements of the science of piloting. First of all, there is one faculty
which a pilot must incessantly cultivate until he has brought it to absolute
perfection. Nothing short of perfection will do. The faculty is memory. He
cannot stop with merely thinking a thing is so and so, he must *know* it, for
this is eminently one of the "exact" sciences. With what scorn a pilot was
looked upon in the old times, if he ever ventured to deal in that feeble
phrase "I think," instead of the vigorous one, "I know!" One cannot
easily realize what a tremendous thing it is to know every trivial detail of
twelve hundred miles of river and know it with absolute exactness. If you
will take the longest street in New York and travel up and down it, con-
ning its features patiently until you know every house and window and
lamppost and big and little sign by heart, and know them so accurately
that you can instantly name the one you are abreast of when you are set
down at random in that street in the middle of an inky black night, you
will then have a tolerable notion of the amount and the exactness of a
pilot's knowledge who carries the Mississippi River in his head. And then,
if you will go on until you know every street-crossing, the character, size,
and position of the crossing-stones, and the varying depth of mud in each

of these numberless places, you will have some idea of what the pilot must know in order to keep a Mississippi steamer out of trouble. Next, if you will take half of the signs in that long street and *change their places* once a month, and still manage to know their new positions accurately on dark nights, and keep up with these repeated changes without making any mistakes, you will understand what is required of a pilot's peerless memory by the fickle Mississippi.*

*Mark Twain, *Life on the Mississippi*, in *The Portable Mark Twain*, ed. Bernard De Voto (New York: Viking Press, Inc., 1956), pp. 109-110.

I think a pilot's memory is about the most wonderful thing in the world. To know the Old and New Testaments by heart and be able to recite them glibly, forward or backward, or begin at random anywhere in the book and recite both ways and never trip or make a mistake, is no extravagant mass of knowledge and no marvelous facility, compared to a pilot's massed knowledge of the Mississippi and his marvelous facility in the handling of it. I make this comparison deliberately, and believe I am not expanding the truth when I do it. Many will think my figure too strong but pilots will not.*

Life on the Mississippi, pp. 110-111.

Exercise 7: Comparison

Write a paragraph that is developed by comparison. Remember that the topic sentence should state the comparison.

CONTRAST

In *TPS* (pp. 10–12), if you remember, we talked about the biggest problem you will have with contrast. We said that unless you swing from side to side in contrast, from *pro* to *con*, your reader is likely to have forgotten about the first side before you finish the second. Obviously, this is less a problem in a paragraph than in a ten-page paper. But even in a paragraph, contrasting point by point is more forceful. Start with a topic sentence and then swing back and forth in paired sentences, one for one side, one for the other. For variety, you might occasionally split a longer paragraph into two, the topic sentence of the first controlling both. But if you do, remember that the two paragraphs together constitute one unit of thought.

Here is an example of a paragraph that moves point by point. And following it is an example (describing the early days of television) of the alternative method:

The most essential distinction between athletics and education lies in the institution's own interest in the athlete as distinguished from its interest in its other students. Universities attract students in order to teach them what they do not already know; they recruit athletes only when they are already proficient. Students are educated for something which will be useful to them and to society after graduation; athletes are required to spend their time on activities the usefulness of which disappears upon graduation or soon thereafter. Universities exist to do what they can for students; athletes are recruited for what they can do for the universities. This makes the operation of the athletic program in which recruited players are used basically different from any educational interest of colleges and universities.*

* Harold W. Stoke, "College Athletics, Education or Show Business?" *Atlantic Monthly,* March 1954, pp. 46-50. Copyright © 1954 by The Atlantic Monthly Company, Boston. Reprinted with permission.

In fact, in some respects the commercials are really better than the shows they sponsor. The commercials are carefully rehearsed, expertly photographed, highly edited and polished. They are made with absolute attention to detail and to the clock. One split-second over time, one bad note, one slightly wrinkled dress and they are done over again. Weeks, even months, go into the production of a single, 60-second commercial.

The shows, on the other hand, are slapped together hastily by writers and performers who have less than a week to put together an hour show. Actors have little time to rehearse, and often the pieces of a show are put together for the first time in front of the camera. Lighting, sound reproduction, and editing are workmanlike, but unpolished; a shadow from an overhead microphone on an actor's face causes no real concern in the control room. A blown line or a muffed cue is "just one of those things that happens." In all, it often takes less time and money to do an hour show than to do the four 60-second commercials that sponsor it.

Exercise 8: Contrast

A. Write a paragraph developed by contrasts. Run your contrasts point by point, using paired sentences.
B. Write two paragraphs of contrast. After the topic sentence, the first should develop one side; the second, parallel to the first in construction, should develop the other side.

DEFINITION

As you write you must sometimes stop to explain your terms. Perhaps a word is unfamiliar, like *telekinesis* or *hubris*. Perhaps you are using a familiar word in an unfamiliar sense: *sophisticated*, meaning "adulterated and artificial"; or *grip*, meaning "stagehand." Sometimes, of course, your explanation may require more than a single paragraph. Sometimes the whole essay becomes an extended definition. But your definitions will usually be single paragraphs to clarify other intentions.

In defining your terms, keep these alternatives in mind:

A. **You can use a single sentence of definition as the topic sentence for your paragraph. (The rest of the paragraph amplifies, explains, and illustrates the topic sentence.) Three sorts of single-sentence definitions are:**

1. *Definition by Synonym.* **A quick way to stipulate the single meaning you want: "Virtue means moral rectitude."**

2. *Definition by Function.* **"A barometer measures atmospheric pressure"— "A social barometer measures human pressures"—"A good quarterback calls the signals and sparks the spirit of the whole team."**

3. *Definition by Synthesis.* **A placing of your term in striking (and not necessarily logical) relationship to its whole class, usually for the purposes of wit: "The fox is the craftiest of beasts"—"A sheep is a friendlier form of goat"—"A lexicographer is a harmless drudge."**

B. **You can use a broader sort of definition than the single-sentence kind mentioned above. Here are three possibilities:**

1. *Definition by Example.* **The opposite of definition by synthesis. You start with the class ("crafty beasts") and then give an example of a member or two ("fox"—plus monkey and raccoon). But of course you would go on to give further examples or illustrations—accounts of how the bacon was snitched through the screen—that broaden your definition beyond the mere naming of class and its members.**

2. *Definition by Comparison.* **Begin with a topic sentence something like: "Love is like the sun." Then extend your comparison on to the end of the paragraph: "Love is like the sun because it gives out warmth, makes everything bright, shines even when it is not seen, and is indeed the center of our lives."**

3. *Definition by Analysis.* **By separating a whole into its parts, you can discover their interrelationships, their natures, and their functions. Definition by analysis is precisely this searching out and probing of the various meanings of a single term.**

Here are four examples of paragraphs of definition:

As the sun was going down, we saw the first specimen of an animal known familiarly over two thousand miles of mountain and desert—from Kansas clear to the Pacific Ocean—as the "jackass rabbit." He is well named. He is just like any other rabbit, except that he is from one third to twice as large, has longer legs in proportion to his size, and has the most preposterous ears that ever were mounted on any creature *but* a jackass. When he is sitting quiet, thinking about his sins, or is absent-minded or unapprehensive of danger, his majestic ears project above him conspicuously; but the breaking of a twig will scare him nearly to death, and then he tilts his ears back gently and starts for home. All you can see, then, for the next minute, is his long gray form stretched out straight and "streaking it" through the low sage-brush, head erect, eyes right, and ears just canted a little to the rear, but showing you where the animal is, all the time, the same as if he carried a jib. Now and then he makes a marvelous spring with his long legs, high over the stunted sage-brush, and scores a leap that would make a horse envious. Presently he comes down to a long, graceful "lope," and shortly he mysteriously disappears. He has crouched behind a sage-bush, and will sit there and listen and tremble until you get within six feet of him, when he will get under way again. But one must shoot at this creature once, if he wishes to see him throw his heart into his heels, and do the best he knows how. He is frightened clear through, now, and he lays his long ears down on his back, straightens himself out like a yard-stick every spring he makes, and scatters miles behind him, with an easy indifference that is enchanting.*

    * Mark Twain, *Roughing It* (New York: Holt, Rinehart and Winston, 1964), pp. 12-13.

    Atheistic existentialism, which I represent, is more coherent. It states that if God does not exist, there is at least one being in whom existence precedes essence, a being who exists before he can be defined by any concept, and that this being is man, or, as Heidegger says, human reality. What is meant here by saying that existence precedes essence? It means that, first of all, man exists, turns up, appears on the scene, and, only afterward, defines himself. If man, as the existentialist conceives him, is indefinable, it is because at first he is nothing. Only afterward will he be something, and he himself will have made what he will be. Thus, there is no human nature, since there is no God to conceive it. Not only is man what he conceives himself to be, but he is also only what he wills himself to be after this thrust toward existence.*

    * Jean Paul Sartre, *Existentialism and Human Emotions* (New York: Philosophical Library, 1957), p. 15.

    Regarded as an idea, democracy is not an alternative to other principles of associated life. It is the idea of community life itself. It is an ideal in the only intelligible sense of an ideal: namely, the tendency and movement of some thing which exists carried to its final limit, viewed as completed, perfected. Since things do not attain such fulfillment but are in actuality distracted and interfered with, democracy in this sense is not a fact and never will be. But neither in this sense is there or has there ever been anything which is a community in its full measure, a community unalloyed by alien elements. The idea or ideal of a community presents, however, actual phases of associated life as they are freed from restrictive and disturbing elements, and are contemplated as having attained their limit of development. Wherever there is conjoint activity whose consequences are appreciated as good by all singular persons who take part in it, and where the realization of the good is such as to effect an energetic desire and effort to sustain it in being just because it is a good shared by all, there is in so far a community. The clear consciousness of a communal life, in all its implications, constitutes the idea of democracy.*

* John Dewey, "Search for the Great Community," *The Public and Its Problems* (New York: Holt, Rinehart and Winston, Inc., 1927), pp. 148-149.

Black Power means, for example, that in Lowndes County, Alabama, a black sheriff can end police brutality. A black tax assessor and tax collector and county board of revenue can lay, collect, and channel tax monies for the building of better roads and schools serving black people. In such areas as Lowndes, where black people have a majority, they will attempt to use power to exercise control. This is what they seek: control. When black people lack a majority, Black Power means proper representation and sharing of control. It means the creation of power bases, of strength, from which black people can press to change local or nation-wide patterns of oppression—instead of from weakness.

It does not mean *merely* putting black faces into office. Black visibility is not Black Power. Most of the black politicians around the country today are not examples of Black Power. The power must be that of a community, and emanate from there. The black politicians must start from there. The black politicians must stop being representatives of "downtown" machines, whatever the cost might be in terms of lost patronage and holiday handouts.*

* Stokely Carmichael and Charles V. Hamilton, *Black Power, the Politics of Liberation in America* (New York: Random House, 1967), p. 15.

Exercise 9. Definition

Write two independent paragraphs defining a term. Use a single-sentence definition (synonym, function, or synthesis) as the topic sentence of the first. Use a broader definition (example, comparison, or analysis) in the second paragraph.

3 The Essay and Paragraph: Tactics of Development

In *TPS*, you have worked with beginning, middle, and end paragraphs for the general essay, and you have probably worked with further exercises in developing these basic paragraphs in Section 2, *Problems*. In addition, you have probably composed several short essays, of three or more paragraphs, bringing these basic paragraphs together in a single coherent whole. Now we will look at a variety of tactics of developing both essays and paragraphs within essays, extending the range surveyed in *TPS*, Chapters 3 and 4, and in *Problems*, Section 2. At the end of this section, we will further consider the problem of coherence within paragraphs, and by extension, essays.

This section begins with exercises in description (space), narration (time), and process to give an added dimension to the discussions and practice in Chapter 4, *TPS*, then proceeds to a discussion and demonstration of various lines of development for both essays and paragraphs that are not touched on directly in *TPS*. But you will see almost at once that these lines, or tactics, of developing essays and paragraphs are simply variations of the theme—developing the standard, or basic, paragraphs for the general essay—already stated in the text (Chapter 3) and in *Problems* (Section 2).

Space   *TPS*, pp. 28–30

You will not often write a purely descriptive essay, because description is ordinarily a part of something larger; it is part of a story, or part of a comparison, or part of an argument. **But if description is ordinarily part of a larger organization, it nonetheless has an inner organization all its own, a spatial organization. It moves left to right, or top to bottom, or front to back, or east to west. In short, it moves through space. Some of the spatial signals are:** *on the right, above, next, across, on the other side, in the front.* **The trick for you as a writer is to choose, to follow, and to make clear to your reader the spatial order most appropriate to your topic.**

Exercise 1: Space

In the exercises that follow, you will find a series of descriptive paragraphs from longer works. In the text of each paragraph, circle words or phrases the author uses as spatial signals. Then, briefly explain on a separate sheet why you think the author chose the particular order he did. What is the "logic" of his organization?

1. The tread on the right front tire was completely worn away, leaving a smooth surface broken only in places by the frayed tire-cord sticking through the rubber. The rim had been dented in several places, and the hub cap was missing. Of the original five, only four lug-nuts held the wheel to the car. Just a few inches in front of the tire, badly bent, was the right half of the front bumper. Much of its chrome had been eaten away by rust, and in one place the metal had been ripped almost halfway through. The fender wasn't much better off. Several sections of the metal were just gone, and what metal remained was covered by highly oxidized and chipped blue paint. Where the headlight had once been mounted, there was now only a rusty hole, and the headlight was precariously fixed to the fender with two metal straps and some masking tape. The turn signal had been broken, and a bare bulb stuck up through the top of the fender. All along the length of the fender where it joined the body there was a corroded and muddy line of rotten metal.

   Resting between the front fenders and covering the engine was a sharply creased and bent hood. In the front, the hood ornament had long since been ripped away, leaving only two rusty holes where it had once been mounted. One of the windshield wipers had disappeared entirely, and the other sagged along the edge of the windshield, half of its rubber segment worn off. The windshield was crazed and clouded with water that had seeped in through the cracks.

2. The Bay of Nukuheva . . . is an expanse of water not unlike in figure the space included within the limits of a horseshoe. It is, perhaps, nine miles in circumference. You approach it from the sea by a narrow entrance, flanked on either side by two small twin islets which soar conically to the height of some five hundred feet. From these the shore recedes on both hands, and describes a deep semicircle.

From the verge of the water the land rises uniformly on all sides, with green and sloping acclivities, until from gentle rolling hillsides and moderate elevations it insensibly swells into lofty and majestic heights, whose blue outlines, ranged all around, close in the view. The beautiful aspect of the shore is heightened by deep and romantic glens, which come down to it at almost equal distances, all apparently radiating from a common center, and the upper extremities of which are lost to the eye beneath the shadow of the mountains. Down each of these little valleys flows a clear stream, here and there assuming the form of a slender cascade, then stealing invisibly along until it bursts upon the sight again in larger and more noisy waterfalls, and at last demurely wanders along to the sea.*

    *Herman Melville, *Typee: A Peep at Polynesian Life During Four Months Residence in a Valley of the Marquesas* (New York: The New American Library of World Literature, Inc., 1964), p. 37.

3. The schoolhouse was a log hut, where Colonel Wheeler used to shelter his corn. It sat in a lot behind a rail fence and thorn bushes, near the sweetest of springs. There was an entrance where a door once was, and

within, a massive rickety fireplace; great chinks between the logs served as windows. Furniture was scarce. A pale blackboard crouched in the corner. My desk was made of three boards, reinforced at critical points, and my chair, borrowed from the landlady, had to be returned every night. Seats for the children—these puzzled me much. I was haunted by a New England vision of neat little desks and chairs, but, alas! the reality was rough plank benches without backs, and at times without legs. They had the one virtue of making naps dangerous,—possibly fatal, for the floor was not to be trusted.*

*W. E. B. DuBois, *The Souls of Black Folk, Essays and Sketches* (Chicago: A. C. McClurg and Company, 1903), p. 57.

4. A few yards from the bench was a high wire fence, too high to leap over, with a curving overhang that made climbing it impossible. Beyond it, a stream—an ordinary, lazy little stream with spring wildflowers along the banks—with nothing to indicate that it divided two worlds. Possibly it was once a river, for its banks were sharply cut and steep. Two Chinese women, in rough gray workclothes and black buns shining, eased their way down its sides in silence, gathering wild yellow lantana. They had an audience: on the other side of the stream a soldier in mustard-colored uniform idly watched them. The sweltering, shrieking harbor of Hong Kong, with its shops of brocade and jade, its opulent hotels and highrise apartments, its tin-shack squatters and child beggars, lay to the southeast only two hours' train distance away. It could have been at the other end of the earth.*

*Lisa Hobbs, *I Saw Red China* (New York: McGraw-Hill Book Company, 1966), pp. 1-2. Used with permission of McGraw-Hill Book Company.

5. Scene. The back room and a section of the bar of Harry Hope's saloon on

an early morning in summer, 1912. The right wall of the back room is a dirty black curtain which separates it from the bar. At rear, this curtain is drawn back from the wall so the bartender can get in and out. The back room is crammed with round tables and chairs placed so close together that it is a difficult squeeze to pass between them. In the middle of the rear wall is a door opening on a hallway. In the left corner, built out into the room, is the toilet with a sign "This is it" on the door. Against the middle of the left wall is a nickel-in-the-slot phonograph. Two windows, so glazed with grime one cannot see through them, are in the left wall, looking out on a backyard. The walls and ceiling once were white, but it was a long time ago, and they are now so splotched, peeled, stained, and dusty that their color can best be described as dirty. The floor, with iron spittoons placed here and there, is covered with sawdust. Lighting comes from single wall brackets, two at left and two at rear.

There are three rows of tables, from front to back. Three are in the front line. The one at left-front has four chairs; the one at center-front, four; the one at right-front, five. At rear of, and half between, front tables one and two is a table of the second row with five chairs. A table, similarly placed at rear of front tables two and three, also has five chairs. The third row of tables, four chairs to one and six to the other, is against the rear wall on either side of the door.*

* Eugene O'Neill, *The Iceman Cometh* in *Selected Plays of Eugene O'Neill* (New York: Random House, Inc., 1969), p. 620.

Time   *TPS,* pp. 30–32

Like space, time is a natural organizer. Again, you simply take your reader along the natural sequence of what happens. We understand processes most clearly by tracking the way they move through time, even processes complicated by other, simultaneous events. You can bring your reader to perceive an event by following the sequence of

things as they happened, stepping aside as necessary to explain background and simultaneous events, guiding your reader along with temporal signposts: *at the same time, now, when, while, then, before, after, next, all the time.*

Exercise 2: Time

In the following exercise you will find a pair of extended prose passages organized according to time. In the text of each essay, circle the words or phrases that signal movement through time. After each essay, comment briefly on the effectiveness of the temporal arrangement.

1. The battle was joined at 3:48 P.M. in a sullen afternoon. Steaming hard, the two battle cruiser forces made contact off the Skagerrak. Hipper immediately reversed course to draw Beatty back upon the main body of the High Seas Fleet. Beatty, always aggressive, followed hard, despite the fact that four fast battleships of his command were well out of range astern. The battle opened at ranges varying from 10,000 to 17,000 yards, with the British ships clear against the western skyline, the German ships dull shapes in the mist to the east. Superior German gunnery and defects in the designs of the British battle cruisers quickly told.

    By 4 P.M. *Tiger* had been hit, and *Lion,* Beatty's flagship, had received its fourth hit from *Lützow.* Q. Turret blew up. Major F. J. W. Harvey of the Royal Marines—both legs severed—ordered the handling room crew to flood the magazines and saved the ship with his dying words. At 4:30 *Indefatigable* disappeared in a terrible sheet of flame and smoke; only two of her crew survived. At 4:06 Sir Hugh Evan-Thomas, with Beatty's four fast battleships, got into the fight at 19,000 yards range, and a 15-inch shell from *Barham* cut through *Von der Tann's* armor and 600 tons of water flooded into the German ship.

    The running fight stood on to the south at twenty-three knots as Hipper led Beatty toward the High Seas Fleet. The *Queen Mary* died at 4:26; a column of smoke mushroomed a thousand feet high and great fluttering clouds of paper, bodies, limbs, turret armor, and a lifeboat were hurled high into the air. Nine men out of 1,275 survived.

Princess Royal took a German salvo and a signalman on *Lion's* flag bridge mistakenly reported her blown up.

Beatty, imperturbable, turned to his flag captain: "Chatfield, there seems to be something wrong with our bloody ships today. Turn two points to port [toward the Germans]."

At 4:50, as the dusk was coming down soon after Scheer's main battle fleet had been sighted, Beatty reversed course to the north, falling back upon Jellicoe in a running fight. Evan-Thomas's tough battleships brought up the rear and gave as good as they received. By 6 P.M. all of *Von der Tann's* guns were out of action, her decks a shambles; *Seydlitz* was afire; *Lützow* and *Derfflinger* seriously damaged.

The sun was low before the main fleets met at last about 6:15 P.M. Squarely across Scheer's course, capping the T of his column, lay the might and majesty of England—*King George V* and *Ajax; Iron Duke* and *St. Vincent; Tremeraire* and *Marlborough; Agincourt* and *Collingwood;* and a host of others bearing proud and ancient names and flying the cross of St. George.

The range was shortened now to 11,000 to 16,000 yards and the British had the advantage of the fading light. At 6:36 Scheer simultaneously reversed the course of his entire fleet—turning southward away from the gaping jaws of the British crescent. But not before he drew blood again; *Invincible,* British battle cruiser, joined the growing company of the departed. Scheer turned north again to the assault at 6:55, partly to try to succor the sinking light cruiser *Wiesbaden* and to aid the crippled *Lützow.* But not for long. His van was the focus for the broadsides of no fewer than thirty-three major British ships. It was too much.

Scheer turned again to southward, covering his retirement with a torpedo attack upon the British battleships. Jellicoe, the cautious, turned his battleships *away* from the torpedoes of the retreating Germans and the main fight was over.*

*Hanson W. Baldwin, *World War I: An Outline History* (New York: Harper & Row, Publishers, Inc., 1962), pp. 89-92. Copyright © 1962 by Hanson W. Baldwin. Reprinted by permission of the publisher.

2. On the evening of the first of March, 1932, an event took place which instantly thrust everything else, even the grim processes of Depression, into the background of American thought—and which seemed to many observers to epitomize cruelly the demoralization into which the country had fallen. The baby son of Colonel and Mrs. Charles A. Lindbergh was kidnapped—taken out of his bed in a second-story room of the new house at Hopewell, New Jersey, never to be seen again alive.

Since Lindbergh's flight to Paris nearly five years before, he had occupied a unique and unprecedented position in American life. Admired almost to the point of worship by millions of people, he was like a sort of uncrowned prince; and although he fiercely shunned publicity, everything he did was so inevitably news that the harder he tried to dodge the limelight, the more surely it pursued him. Word that he had been seen anywhere was enough to bring a crowd running; he was said to have been driven at times to disguise himself in order to be free of mobbing admirers. He now occupied himself as a consultant in aviation; late the preceding summer he and his wife, the former Anne Morrow, had made a "flight to the Orient" which Mrs. Lindbergh later described in lovely prose; and since his meeting with Dr. Alexis Carrel late in 1930 he had begun experiments in the construction of perfusion pumps which were to bring him a high reputation as a biological technician. His new house at Hopewell, remote and surrounded by woods, had been built largely as a retreat in which the Lindberghs could be at peace from an intrusive world.

And now, suddenly, this peace was shattered. Within a few hours of the discovery that the Lindbergh baby's bed was empty—the blankets still held in place by their safety pins—a swarm of police and newspaper men had reached the house and were trampling about the muddy grounds, obliterating clues. And when the news broke in the next morning's news-papers, the American people went into a long paroxysm of excitement.*

* Frederick Lewis Allen, *Since Yesterday: The Nineteen-Thirties in America* (New York: Harper & Row, Publishers, Inc.), pp. 67-69. Copyright 1939, 1940 by Harper & Row, Publishers, Inc. Reprinted by permission of the publisher.

Process   *TPS*, pp. 33–34

You saw in *TPS*, p. 34, that even a simple description of a process can take a quite sharp argumentative edge. But to be effective, whether argumentative or not, a description of a process must be put in words the reader can quickly absorb, and its parts must be in an order the reader can perceive with little effort. In the exercises of Chapter 4 of *TPS*, you may have already struggled to bring clarity and order to a description of your own; in the following exercises, you have an opportunity to clear another's muddle, and to choose between two descriptions of the same process, justifying your choice.

Exercise 3: Process

Look over the following passage. Obviously, the description is muddy—irrelevant statements, limp humor, and, most important, a poor sequence of facts and procedures. Make this description as clear as the distillate from the blanket, and try to retain a light touch, too.

THE BLANKET STILL

The most important method of distillation is by use of the blanket still. It is used to distill herbal medicines, love potions, and spiritous liquors. Its use was lost in antiquity for no one knows how long. Hundreds of years, maybe, and perhaps thousands.

You need two bowls and a blanket first you fill the larger bowl with water but only about half full and then you float the smaller bowl with herbal material or mash in the water in the larger bowl. The worker then covered the bowl with a blanket or other kind of cloth.

In Scotland, the men covered the bowls with their kilts.

You next get the water in the larger bowl hot enough to make the material in the smaller bowl boil. The water didn't boil but the material in the smaller bowl will because it boiled at a lower temperature than water. One hundred and fifty degrees rather than 212 degrees, the boiling point of water. The material in the smaller bowl, a liquid, of course, will condense again in the blanket or piece of cloth stretched across the top of both bowls. The worker took the blanket off the bowls just before the water began to boil in the bigger bowl then you squeeze the blanket and out comes a pure distillate free of all material other than what you want. The worker squeezed the blanket into a third bowl, of course, although when the Scots made whiskey with a blanket still they couldn't wait but used to whip the kilt off the hot pot and chew it.*

Adapted from Peter B. Ross, *Basic Technical Writing* (New York: Thomas Y. Crowell Co., 1974), p. 37.

Exercise 4: Process

Both the following accounts, about the discovery of the structure of nucleic acid, appeared on March 19, 1965, the first in the *New York Times,* **and the second in the** *Syracuse Post-Standard.** **Which is most likely to be understood by the average reader? Which account do you prefer? Write a short essay analyzing your choice. Hint: in your analysis, consider the structure of the sentences in each account, compare vocabularies, and comment on the definitions and on the order of facts and processes in each account.**

1. The nucleic acid whose structure those scientists have worked out represents one of four kinds in a living cell.

   One is deoxyribonucleic acid, or DNA. This is the genetic material in whose structure are encoded the hereditary instructions that make every living organism the way it is.

   That is accomplished through the replication and transmission from cell generation to cell generation of the DNA and through the direction by DNA of the synthesis of three kinds of ribonucleic acid, or RNA. Those RNA's in turn direct the manufacture of the workhorse molecules of life, proteins.

   One of the three RNA's is called messenger. It carries the hereditary instructions for protein synthesis to minute "protein factories," called ribosomes, in the cell. There amino acids are strung together into chain-like protein molecules. Ribosomes are made of the second kind of ribonucleic acid, ribosomal RNA.

   The third form of ribonucleic acid is called "transfer RNA" because it transfers amino acids from the cell fluid to the ribosomes for assembly into proteins according to the instructions borne there from DNA by messenger RNA.

2. Most diseases, moreover, involve protein molecules and a disruption of the protein-making process. The big problem for medical researchers has been in recognizing just what happens inside a protein when disease attacks. They couldn't tell because they did not know enough about the protein manufacture process.

   This is where the new key found by Cornell scientists comes in.

   Using some chemical wizardry, the group of researchers, headed by Dr. Robert W. Holley, teased from some cells an extract of "alinine transfer RNA." This is a molecule which ferries the amino acid alinine to the protein assembly line where it goes into the bigger molecule.

   They put it through a series of purifying steps to get an uncontaminated product, and then started to probe its architecture, brick by brick. This is the usual way biochemists work. To know how a cell

* Quoted in Andre Fontaine, *The Art of Writing Nonfiction* (New York: Thomas Y. Crowell Co., 1974), pp. 246-247.

works they've got to take out each component, clean it up, study it in detail and determine its place in the total picture.

They found the substance was constructed of 77 smaller molecular bits arranged in a definite sequence—something like a 77-letter word. Another type of transfer RNA would have a different letter sequence spelling out a shorter or longer word and do a different job.

Thus, for the first time, the actual structure of a transfer RNA molecule was revealed.

Cause and Effect

Your success at handling the orders of space and of time depends to a good degree upon your skill as an observer. If you have good eyes, ears, and memory, you should —with practice—be able to answer the questions, "What haappened?" or "What does it look like?" This is not to say that description and narration are easy. If you have ever tried to find a reliable witness to a fender-bending accident, you know how wild our recollections can be! But if you stay alert and keep your reader in mind, your natural senses of space and of time should provide effective substance and organization for your writing.

When we come to the cause-and-effect method of organizing the middle of an essay, or whole essay, our thought is more complex. Here we start in the present with an effect and try to work back into the past to discover its probable causes. Or we start with the cause and try to look forward into the future to discover its eventual effects. In either case, we start with the observation of a present fact, and we add to it speculation about what has come before or what will come after. In short, to the skills of the observer, we add the skills of the analyst, the investigator, the logician.

But if the thoughts in cause-and-effect writing are more complex than those in descriptive and narrative writing, the organization of cause-and-effect essays is actually quite simple. You really have only two possibilities. In Arrangement I, you start with a known effect and then attempt to identify its causes. "North of the Tracks" in *TPS*, pp. 24, 26, is a good example of Arrangement I. In Arrangement II, you start with a known cause and then attempt to predict its probable effects. Arrangement I looks to the past; Arrangement II looks to the future. For example, the following paragraph from a report by *Time* magazine on Fred Hoyle, the British astronomer and mathematician who has been modifying Newton's gravity and Einstein's relativity, states the general condition, proposes its hypothetical cause with an *if*, then moves to the future effects, first in temporal order and then in order of human interest:

The masses, and therefore the gravity, of the sun and the earth are partly due to each other, partly to more distant objects such as the stars and galaxies. According to Hoyle, if the universe were to be cut in half, local solar-system gravitation would double, drawing the earth closer to the sun. The pressure in the sun's center would increase, thus raising its temperature, its generation of energy, and its brightness. Before being seared into a lump of charcoal, a man on earth would find his weight increasing from 150 to 300 lb.

But keep one thing in mind: the basic principle of organizing the middle section of an essay is that you should move from the least important to the most important. The same thing applies here. Let us say you start with a cause, and, after careful analysis, you are convinced that there will be four probable results from this cause. The least significant of these effects should come first in your essay, and then the more significant of those effects. Finish with what you think to be the most certain and the most significant of the four effects. If, on the other hand, you are starting with an effect and trying to work back to its causes, you will likely discover that some of the causes are only contributory while others are immediate. Some of the causes are simple *conditions,* **while others are** *immediate causes.* **Again the principle is the same. Start with the conditions, or lesser causes, and move to the immediate causes, or the greater causes.**

Exercise 5: Cause and Effect

Below is a list of statements (applicable until the recent recession) about the population of the United States, some general, some particular. First arrange them in a suitable order for Arrangement I, then arrange them again in a suitable order for Arrangement II. Remember that subordinate points should also follow the order of ascending importance.

1. An expanding population quickly expends resources and energy for new housing, and often neglects existing housing.
2. The annual death rate has declined slightly since 1940 (a decrease of slightly over one death per thousand of population).
3. Increasing population overstrains the classrooms in public schools, and has already forced enlarged classes and, in some instances, half-day sessions.
4. Despite our more recent concern and awareness, the total population of the United States has continued to increase since the mid-1940's.
5. The annual birth rate per thousand of population has declined (15.6 in 1972 compared with the 1960 rate of 23.7). Nevertheless, 3.3 million babies were born in 1972, almost exactly the same number as twenty years previously.
6. An increasing population strains college facilities; the number of college students doubled between 1960 and 1970 and may be half again as large by 1980.
7. Immigration has gradually increased in recent years (385,000 in 1972 compared with 292,000 in 1964).
8. An expanding population forces cities to fill land once used for recreation and crops with shopping centers, streets, and houses.
9. An expanding population eventually crowds more people into less space, increasing their vulnerability to disease, to squalor, and to strife.

Problem and Solution

With problem-and-solution, you again exploit a natural order. You describe the problem for your reader; you then suggest solutions. This order serves well even for historical subjects. The Panama Canal, for instance, posed problems of politics, geology, and human survival. Your thesis would state the threefold problem; your middle would show its three solutions, one by one. Or you might choose a more obviously balanced approach, making your thesis "The Canal posed three major problems," and then organizing your middle in two equal parts:

I. The problems
   A. Difficulties of agreement between a small government and a large one
   B. Difficulties with variations in terrain and differing sea levels
   C. Yellow fever
II. The solutions
   A. The Canal Zone, sovereignty, payments
   B. Distance, lakes, and locks
   C. General Gorgas and the mosquito

This topic could expand into a considerable essay, complete with footnotes, but it also might turn out nicely in three paragraphs, based on articles in the *Encyclopaedia Britannica:*

DIGGING THE PANAMA CANAL

Dig this! The idea of the Panama Canal is almost as old as Columbus. When the Spanish explorers finally conceded that any passage westward to China, which Columbus had sought, was blocked by two continents and a thin isthmus, the idea of a canal was born. In 1550, Antonio Galvão began the long argument for a canal through Nicaragua, Panama, or Darien. When the United States opened the canal on August 15, 1914, the dreams of almost four centuries came true, and mountainous problems had been solved. Ultimately, the canal had posed three major problems.

Politics, geology, and human survival had confronted canal-planners from the beginning. A French company, organized in 1880 to dig the canal, repeatedly had to extend its treaties at higher and higher prices as the work dragged on. Uneasy about the French, the United States made treaties with Nicaragua and Costa Rica to dig along the other most feasible route. This political threat, together with the failure of the French and the revolt of Panama from Colombia, finally enabled the United States to buy the French rights and negotiate new treaties, which, nevertheless, continue to cause political trouble to this day. Geology also posed its ancient problems: how to manage torrential rivers and inland lakes; whether to build a longer but more enduring canal at sea level, or a shorter, cheaper, and safer canal with locks. Economy eventually won, but the problem of yellow fever and malaria, which had plagued the French, remained. By detecting and combating the fever-carrying mosquito, William Gorgas solved these ancient tropical problems. Without him, the political and geological solutions would have come to nothing.

In the end, of course, all three problems are human, as the canal answered the ancient human dream of a westward passage to China. Political tensions are nothing but human competition, and geology succumbs to human drives. And to dig a canal through the jungle, man had to triumph over the mosquito. The victories over the terrain and the mosquito remain virtually complete. But the ancient commercial impulse, which launched the idea of the canal in the first place, and the political tensions, which include the worldwide launching of larger navies with atomic submarines, continue to surround the old incision across the Isthmus of Panama.

Any problem and its solutions can produce an essay along these lines—choosing a college or something to wear (if you want to be light-hearted), making an apartment or a commune work, building the Eiffel Tower or the pyramids.

Exercise 6: Problem and Solution

Posing a problem (or problems) and solution, write a two- or three-paragraph paper in which you describe some particularly interesting architectural or engineering accomplishment. Choose any topic you wish. For example, how did architects design the high-rise buildings in San Francisco so that they could withstand the shock of the severe earthquakes of 1971? Or how did medieval man make a suit of armor? Or how do you plan to convert your VW bus into a camper that will sleep four people? In the first paragraph, state the problem. Then go on to describe how the problem could be, or was, solved.

Natural Divisions

Many subjects fall into natural or customary partitions, which supply you with a kind of dialectic contrast (such as *pro-con*) not necessarily hostile, and even blandly jointed, like a good roast of pork, ready for carving: freshman, sophomore, junior, senior; Republicans, Democrats; right, middle, left; legislative, executive, judicial. Similarly, any manufacturing process, or any machine, will already have distinct steps and parts. These customary divisions will help your reader, since he knows something of them already. Mention the Democratic position on inflation, and he will naturally expect your description of the Republican position to follow. If no other divisions suggest themselves, you can often divide your essay into a consistent series of parallel answers, or "reasons for," or "reasons against"—something like this:

A broad liberal education is best:

I. It prepares you for a world of changing employment.
II. It enables you to function well as a citizen.
III. It enables you to make the most of your life.

Exercise 7: Natural Divisions

Here are a number of topics that fall conveniently into natural divisions. For each topic, list the divisions that occur to you as if you were organizing an essay around the topic.

1. Causes affecting the rate at which a population grows.
2. Levels of government.
3. The "lunatic-fringe."
4. The early stages of space technology.
5. Undersea exploration.
6. Geological eras.
7. Mathematics in public schools.
8. Governmental response to the Depression.
9. Defrauding insurance companies.
10. Inequities in the tax structure.

Induction

For most papers, particularly for long papers, the reader needs your thesis at the beginning, so that he knows where you are taking him, or why he is reading the paper, or what he will get out of it, as if you had given him a road map and pointed out your destination. You say, "Here's where we are going; now, let's go back to the starting point and see how we can get there." The advantage of this order obviously is clarity. Your reader knows what to expect. For an occasional short paper, however, both you and your reader may enjoy turning this usual deductive order around. Thus, instead of starting with your conclusion, you lead up to it—as if you said, "Let's start out on this road and see where we end up." Because your reader is not entirely certain where he is going, he enjoys an air of suspense. You keep him just a little in doubt as you lead him along towards your conclusion. But don't stretch too far. Too long a suspense may sag into befuddlement. Remember, deduction for clarity; induction for suspense.

Exercise 8: Induction

Write a one-paragraph inductive essay in which you use this format. Start with a question. Then, dismissing partial answers, lead your reader to your main and conclusive point. ("What is A? It might be B, and I know a lot of people think it is C,

but I think it is really D.") Here is an example taken from an interview with a man reminiscing about his experiences during the Depression:

> What was the worst thing about the Depression? Well, I don't know. I guess for some folks it was losing their savings. For us that wasn't so bad. I only had about $400 in the McLain County Bank when it closed and I got some of that back later, about 10 cents on the dollar. Then too, being out of work was rough for a lot of people. But even that wasn't so bad for me. I lost my job with the coal company in 1931, but we lived on a farm. And with that and some odd jobs I picked up, I managed to keep pretty busy until I got a steady job again. Of course, I know a lot of people didn't have enough to eat or enough to wear during the Depression. For us that wasn't too bad. We grew most of our own food, and my wife is pretty handy at sewing, so we got by. Nothing very fancy, you understand, but we managed. No, I guess for us the worst thing about the Depression was we got to feeling after a while that times just weren't ever going to get better. It just went on too long. For us, things got a little rough in 1930 and they stayed pretty rough until I got a job with the Highway Commission in 1938. Eight years is a long time to keep hoping. It just went on so long.

Deduction

By this time, you know the deductive order, even if not its name. It is precisely the same "thesis-first" structure we have examined in Chapters 1 and 2 in *TPS* and in Chapter 1 in *Problems*. Here, you lead away from your general proposition. You start with your thesis and then explain it, defend it, prove it.

Exercise 9: Deduction

In the previous exercise, you wrote a one-paragraph paper using inductive order. Now try turning that paper around so that you transform it into a deductive paper. Begin with a thesis to be demonstrated rather than with a question to be answered. You might find, by the way, that in switching the paper from inductive to deductive order it will tend to grow a bit. If so, fine; let it grow. Here is an example:

> For most Americans, the stock market crash was not the worst thing about the Depression. True, it carried away billions of dollars of investors' money, but relatively few of us felt directly affected. Few of us owned stock, and for most of us the market collapse was something that happened to other people, not to us. Of course, as we found out, the stock market collapse was only the trigger, and soon more and more Americans found their lives directly affected. By 1932, 25 percent of the work force was without jobs. Yet, for many Americans, the worst thing about the

Depression was not the bank closures, or being out of work, or even shortages of food and clothing. For many of us, the worst thing about the Depression was that it lasted so long we almost gave up hoping that times would ever get better. George Harris of Wellsburg, West Virginia, is a good example of how the Depression hit most of us.

In 1931, Mr. Harris had a job with the Green Coal Company as a tender on a boat that pushed coal barges up and down the Ohio River. His income was generally pretty good, and Mr. Harris had managed to buy a small farm just outside town. But cutbacks in industrial production, particularly in the production of steel, soon forced cutbacks in coal mining as well. And in August of 1931, Mr. Harris was laid off. The next year, in 1932, the McLain County Bank closed, and with it went the only savings the Harrises had, $400, although later he did manage to collect 10 percent of his lost savings. And so for the next seven years, Mr. Harris bounced from job to job, whatever he could get: a few days here, a few days there. He was thus able to hold onto his small farm, and on it he raised most of the food for the Harris family for the next seven years. Mrs. Harris, too, helped to cut corners by making most of the family's clothes, and by repairing things when they wore out. In this way, taking it one day at a time, and living as simply and as frugally as possible, the Harrises managed to get by until, in 1938, Mr. Harris once again got a secure and well-paying job with the County Road Commission.

So the Harrises are a good example of how the Depression hit many Americans. They lost some savings, they lost their jobs, they had to tighten their belts, but they managed to get by. For them, the worst thing about the Depression was not the deprivation; it was simply that the Depression went on year after year. As Mr. Harris says, "Eight years is a long time to keep hoping. It just went on so long."

Deduction-Induction

Very few of the essays you write will be purely inductive. The order just is not well suited to long or complex papers. But some papers can remain essentially inductive within a basically deductive framework. This sort of paper usually begins with a very broadly stated assertion or with a question that partially suggests an answer. The opening tells us what to expect, but only generally. The *real* answer to the question, or the *real* statement of the thesis does not occur until the end of the paper. This order, the deductive-inductive order, combines the advantages of each of the two individual orders. It combines the clarity of the deductive order with the suspense of the inductive order.

Exercise 10: Deduction-Induction

Here are two essays in which the internal movement is essentially inductive. That is, the stress tends to fall at the end of the essay rather than at the beginning. In one

of the two essays, however, an initial deductive framework helps to clarify the writer's central proposition, to give us a preview of the thesis before the paper's conclusion drives home his main idea. Read the two essays, and then answer the questions that follow.

THE SIGNS OF A GOOD GOVERNMENT

When, therefore, one asks what in absolute terms is the best government, one is asking a question which is unanswerable because it is indeterminate; or alternatively one might say that there are as many good answers as there are possible combinations in the absolute and relative positions of peoples.

But if it is asked by what signs one can tell whether a given people is well or badly governed, that is another matter; and the question of fact can be answered.

Even so, it is not really answered, because everyone will want to answer it in his own way. Subjects prize public tranquillity; citizens the freedom of the individual—the former prefer security of possessions, the latter security of person; subjects think the best government is the most severe, citizens that it is the mildest; the former want crimes to be punished, the latter want them prevented; subjects think it is a good thing to be feared by their neighbours, citizens prefer to be ignored by them; the former are satisfied so long as money circulates, the latter demand that the people shall have bread. But even if there were agreement on these and suchlike points, should we be any more advanced? Moral dimensions have no precise standard of measurement; even if we could agree about signs, how should we agree in appraisal?

For myself, I am always astonished that people should fail to recognize so simple a sign, or be so insincere as not to agree about it. What is the object of any political association? It is the protection and the prosperity of its members. And what is the surest evidence that they are so protected and prosperous? The numbers of their population. Then do not look beyond this much debated evidence. All other things being equal, the government under which, without external aids like naturalization and immigration, the citizens increase and multiply most, is infallibly the best government. That under which the people diminishes and wastes away is the worst. Statisticians, this is your problem: count, measure, compare.*

    * Jean-Jacques Rousseau, *The Social Contract*, translated by Maurice Cranston (New York: Penguin Books, 1968), pp. 129-130. Reprinted by permission of A.D. Peters and Company, Ltd., London.

HOW CITIES OR STATES PREVIOUSLY INDEPENDENT
MUST BE GOVERNED AFTER OCCUPATION

When those states which have been accustomed to live in freedom under their own laws are acquired, there are three ways of trying to keep them. The first is to destroy them, the second to go and live therein, and the third to allow them to continue to live under their own laws, taking a tribute from them and creating within them a new government of a few which will keep the state friendly to you. For since such a government is the creature of the prince it will know that it cannot exist without his friendship and authority and is thus certain to do its best to support him, and a city accustomed to freedom can be more easily held through its citizens than in any other way if it is desired to preserve it. Here we have the examples of the Spartans and the Romans. The Spartans held Athens and Thebes and created in both a government of a few; nonetheless they lost them. The Romans, in order to hold Capua, Carthage, and Numantia, razed them and did not lose them. They tried to keep Greece in the same way the Spartans had, permitting the country to be free under its own laws, but in this they were not successful inasmuch as they were compelled to destroy many cities of that province in order to hold it, for in truth there is no sure way of holding them other than by their ruin. And whoever becomes master of a city accustomed to living in freedom and does not destroy it may expect to be destroyed by it himself, for it has always as an incentive to rebellion the name of liberty and its own ancient laws which neither time nor favors received can cause the citizens to forget. And whatever action be taken or provision be made, as long as the inhabitants are not separated or dispersed, that name and those laws are never forgotten but provide a rallying point in every emergency, as is shown by the case of Pisa after many years of subjection to the Florentines. Cities or provinces used to living under a prince are accustomed to obedience, and when the ruling house becomes extinct they are unable to agree on a successor and, having no experience of self-government, they are slow in taking up arms and so with greater ease a prince may overcome them and feel secure in his possession of them. In republics there is greater life, greater hatred, more desire of vengeance, and the memory of their ancient liberty gives them no rest; so the safest way is either to extinguish them or go and live in them.*

*Niccolo Machiavelli, *The Prince*, translated and edited by Thomas G. Bergin (Arlington Heights, Ill.: AHM Publishing Corporation, 1947), pp. 12-13. Copyright © 1947 by AHM Publishing Corporation. Reprinted by permission of the publisher.

1. What is Rousseau's thesis?
2. Do you find any anticipations of the thesis in the paper's opening section?
3. What is Machiavelli's thesis?
4. What anticipations of his thesis do you find in his opening section?
5. Which of these two seems to be the deductive-inductive essay?

Coherence

We have looked briefly at several ways of developing paragraphs and essays. In *TPS*, we have seen paragraphs developed by description, by narration, by illustration, by citing authority, by comparison, by contrast, and by definition, and in this chapter we have worked with more tactics of developing both paragraphs and essays. Of course, these are not all the options open to you, but these methods of development will provide you with a good start; from there you can experiment and discover other ways for yourself. One more point, however, includes the others: making paragraphs stick together, that is, coherence.

In large measure, of course, coherence is the natural result of finding your own voice, acknowledging a specific audience, and being completely clear about what you want to do. When you have done those three things, coherence is not something you have to seek; it happens. Your ideas and examples will lead the reader along easily, each paragraph serving as a stepping-stone to the next, and each paragraph, within itself, a smooth and coherent unit of thought. Coherence is no editorial trick, no last-minute patching to hide the cracks. It is the external reflection of an internal unity.

But we all *think* our writing has unity. "After all," we say, "it's perfectly clear to me. Why wouldn't it be clear to someone else?" Yet we all know from sad experience that it is not always clear to someone else. So check your writing—paragraph and whole essay—for signs of incoherence. Here are seven common flaws to look for:

1. Inadequate topic sentence (for paragraphs).
2. Insufficient detail.
3. Insufficient transitional tags.
4. Infrequent repetition of key terms.
5. Shifting point of view.
6. Inconsistent order.
7. Interruptions for parenthetical comment.

Exercise 11: Coherence

Below is a short excerpt from W. E. B. DuBois's *The Souls of Black Folk* in which he is describing the "Black Belt" of Georgia as he saw it in 1903. Read this paragraph, and then answer the questions that follow it.

It is a land of rapid contrasts and of curiously mingled hope and pain. Here sits a pretty blue-eyed quadroon hiding her bare feet; she was married only last week, and yonder in the field is her dark young husband, hoeing to support her, at thirty cents a day without board. Across the way is Gatesby, brown and tall, lord of two thousand acres shrewdly won and held. There is a store conducted by his black son, a blacksmith shop, and a ginnery. Five miles below here is a town owned and controlled by one white New Englander. He owns almost a Rhode Island county, with thousands of acres and hundreds of black laborers. Their cabins look better than most, and the farm, with machinery and fertilizers, is much more business-like than any in the county, although the manager drives hard bargains in wages. When now we turn and look five miles above, there on the edge of town are five houses of prostitutes,—two of blacks and three of whites; and in one of the houses of the whites a worthless black boy was harbored too openly two years ago; so he was hanged for rape. And here, too, is the high whitewashed fence of the "stockade," as the county prison is called; the white folks say it is ever full of black criminals,—the black folks say that only colored boys are sent to jail, and they not because they are guilty, but because the State needs criminals to eke out its income by their forced labor.*

* W. E. B. DuBois, *The Souls of Black Folk, Essays and Sketches* (Chicago: A. C. McClurg & Co., 1903), pp. 125-126.

1. What sort of paragraph is this?
2. What is the topic sentence of the paragraph?
3. What details support the topic sentence? Be specific.
4. Do these details follow a consistent order? Give examples to support your answer.
5. What transitional tags are there?
6. Does DuBois repeat key terms? If so, which and where?
7. Is the point of view consistent? If so, describe it.
8. Does the author interrupt his paragraph with parenthetical comments?
9. What do you think are the clearest evidences of coherence within this paragraph?

Exercise 12: Coherence

Supply one sample paragraph from your own writing. Choose a paragraph from a paper you have already done, or, if you wish, write a new paragraph. Choose a paragraph you think rather good, one you think coherent. Then answer the following questions:

1. What sort of paragraph is this?
2. What is the topic sentence of the paragraph?
3. What details support your topic sentence?
4. Do these details follow a consistent order?
5. What transitional tags are there?
6. Do you repeat key terms?
7. Is your point of view consistent?
8. Do you interrupt your paragraph with parenthetical comments?
9. What do you think are the clearest evidences of coherence within this paragraph?

4 Sentences

Perhaps we seem to be going backward, turning—as we are—to sentences just after we have finished discussing paragraphs. But in writing a paper, you *do* work backward. You start with only a vague notion of what you want to do. Next, you try to develop both a clear statement of that idea and a plan that will help you to develop it. Then, you rough out the paper, perhaps more than once, adding ideas and examples as they present themselves. And not until all this has happened, not until you are satisfied the rough draft *is* workable, do you go back for a close look at your sentences. Writing is rather like building a house: you do not start with the trimming; you start with the foundation and the roughed-in carpentry. So, although you write a paper one sentence at a time, you probably do not come to the business of carefully revising those sentences until close to the end of the whole process. Therefore, we are going "backward" because this is how you actually write your paper. Rough it out first; *then* go back to clean it up for public appearance.

Let us start with a review of the variety of sentences you have to work with. English has two. They are the loose, or strung-along sentence, and the periodic sentence. The loose sentence is strung along from subject through verb to object, with whatever else just added as it comes to mind. *John hit Joe. John unexpectedly hit Joe. John unexpectedly hit Joe a roundhouse punch.* The periodic sentence, on the other hand, delays completing its meaning until the very end. Carefully contrived for suspense, it holds off giving you all the parts until the last word has been reached. *John, the best student in the class and usually the quietest, hit Joe.* The loose sentence moves straight along: subject, verb, object. The periodic sentence, on the other hand, suspends its whole meaning until the end.

Now, with those two terms in mind, let us look, one at a time, at each of the common patterns of the English sentence: the simple sentence, the compound sentence, and the complex sentence. Bear in mind our object is to help you revise your first draft so it is polished, clear, and precise.

Simple Sentences

TPS, p. 45

Learn to use strong, active verbs; *John hit Joe,* **not** *Joe was hit by John.* **This has two advantages. First, it will give your sentences the energy stored up in a good, gutsy verb.** *He groaned,* **for example, has far more energy than its trite passive equivalent,** *A groan issued from his lips.* **Second, active verbs will avoid the twisted and wordy orders the passive verb requires, and reduce the number of words. For example, the sentence** *He groaned* **has just two words; its passive counterpart,** *A groan issued from his lips,* **has six. Same idea, three times as many words. You can cut the sentence** *It was suggested by the manager that cuts be made in spending* **from twelve words to six simply by switching to active verbs:** *The manager suggested we cut spending.* **Active verbs always have more energy than passives, and they will eliminate many dull and useless words.**

Next, learn to give your simple sentences a touch of periodicity. You can do that in several ways: change the normal "subject-verb-object" word order. *The house itself she hated, but the yard was grand.* **Or, insert interruptive words or phrases to delay the normal working out of the sentence.** *The manuscript, especially, he treasured.* **This sentence has a touch more suspense than its conventional form:** *He especially treasured the manuscript.* **Finally, complicate any one of the three elements: subject, verb, or object.**

> **The subject:** *King Lear, proud, old, and childish, probably aware that his grip on the kingdom is beginning to slip, devises a foolish plan.*
>
> **Or the verb:** *Carefully at first, then confidently, then with reckless steps, she made her way along the peak of the smoldering roof.*
>
> **Or the object:** *Her notebooks contain marvelous comments on the turtle in the back yard, the flowers and weeds, the great elm by the drive, the road, the earth, the stars, and the men and women of the village.*

Exercise 1: Simple Sentences

In the following exercise, you will find a list of simple sentences. Eliminate their wordiness; activate their verbs.

1. The Bowen Company made an estimate that the sewer project would have a cost of $450,000.

____

____

____

____

2. The assembly department made an attempt to achieve more production by getting the advice of a time-and-motion expert.

____

____

____

3. I feel admiration for the student who can do intensive studying despite the 90-degree temperatures.

____

____

____

4. Space scientists have to take the man-made radiation belt into consideration when the orbits of satellites are plotted.

____

____

____

____

5. The sewage system needs enlargement if it is to meet the needs of the city in the next ten years.

____

____

____

6. No serious, industry-wide effort has been made to effect the standardization of plumbing fixtures.

____

____

____

7. A variety of federal and state energy commissions and some large electrical utilities are making studies of the technical feasibility and the safety of nuclear power plants that are capable of production of 1 million kilowatts.

____

____

____

____

8. The chief work of this course is the development of a design for a light plane.

____

____

____

9. Preliminary investigation showed that failure of pump bearings occurred in all cases.

____

____

____

10. This company is engaged in the manufacture of hi-fi components.

____

____

11. The examination of the candidates was conducted by the security officer.

____

____

____

12. Announcement of results will occur when a decision has been reached by the panel of judges

13. Revision of the chart of organization should be an annual concern of the board of directors.

14. Detonation of the mixture occurred when a cigarette was accidentally dropped onto the workbench by one of the observers.

15. The failure of this student is attributable to his insufficient study.

Exercise 2: Simple Sentences

Cull through your papers and find five simple sentences with passive verbs. As above, revise them.

Exercise 3: Simple Sentences

Give each of the following sentences a touch of periodicity by changing the normal word order, by adding interruptive words or phrases, or by complicating one of the three principal elements of the sentence: the subject, the verb, the object.

1. (Example) She made her way along the smoldering roof. Carefully at first,

then confidently, then with reckless steps, she made her way along the peak of the smoldering roof.

2. The editorial in the *New York Times* suggested that tight control of government spending might check inflation.

____

____

____

3. It was wholly unlike his father to give up without trying.

____

____

4. The inspector discovered a window that had been forced open.

____

____

5. We certainly remember that first night in the new house!

____

____

6. The escaped convict offered only token resistance and allowed himself to be captured and disarmed after a short chase by a private citizen.

____

____

____

7. William Faulkner died of a heart attack on July 6, 1962.

____

____

8. The *Scientific American* customarily devotes its September issue to a single, unified topic.

____

____

____

9. We must note that some parents have misgivings about the schools.

____

____

10. The house sits at the edge of town in the middle of large grounds.

____

____

Exercise 4: Simple Sentences

Cull through your papers again and find five of your own simple sentences. Then revise them as in Exercise 3.

Compound Sentences *TPS*, pp. 45–47

A compound sentence is nothing more than a pair of simple sentences linked together in one of four ways:

1. **By coordinating conjunctions:** *and, but, or, nor.* **Put a comma before the conjunction.**

2. **By conjunctive adverbs:** *therefore, moreover, however, nevertheless, consequently, furthermore.* **Put a semicolon before, a comma after.**

3. **By one of the "in-betweeners":** *yet, still, so*—**adverbs that can serve a conjunctive function. Put either a semicolon or a comma before any of these, depending upon the degree of emphasis you want (see** *TPS*, **p. 47).**

4. **By a semicolon or comma alone. Save the comma for those rare instances in which you have two or three very short and closely related sentences to join. Otherwise use the semicolon.**

Exercise 5: Compound Sentences

In the following exercise, you will find fifteen pairs of simple sentences. Turn them

into compounds with the coordinator you think most appropriate to the sense and style of the sentences. Then, beside each sentence, indicate the other coordinators you *could* have chosen.

1. He couldn't go on. He was just too tired.

   ____

2. The crime commission recommended a number of such programs. Federal funds have been made available for putting them into operation.

   ____

   ____

   ____

3. The governor advised the President that the state was unable to cope with the disaster. The President issued a proclamation to dispatch federal troops.

   ____

   ____

   ____

   ____

4. The first plant generating electricity by reactor began operating in 1956. Nuclear technology has been growing rather slowly since then.

   ____

   ____

   ____

   ____

5. We can probably never perfect the process beyond its present state. We should still try.

   ____

   ____

6. In some instances, the seminar for freshman courses would be extremely helpful. In other instances, it might be of little value.

7. The thought of quitting his job excited him. The idea had been in the back of his mind for a long time.

8. Most schools are just now starting courses in computers for freshmen. To evaluate those programs will take several years.

9. In his manuscripts, F. Scott Fitzgerald's sentences are often haphazard and careless. His spelling is often atrocious.

10. On small farms, labor was not specialized. On medium farms, labor was partially specialized. But on large farms workers were carefully divided into teams of specialists.

11. Few recipients of Social Security benefits can actually live on that income alone. Most supplement their incomes with savings or by selling the possessions of a lifetime.

---

12. Mark Twain's book, *The Gilded Age*, attempts too much. It attempts to satirize an age.

---

13. Within the past three years, jobs open to recent graduates have steadily shrunk. As a result, students are increasingly challenging the curriculum to provide them marketable skills.

---

14. We have made some progress in controlling exhaust. We still have a long way to go.

---

15. Statistically, your chances of being killed or injured in an airplane are far lower than in an automobile. Most of us, however, are more nervous in planes than in cars.

Exercise 6: Compound Sentences

In your own writing, find five likely pairs of simple sentences and link them together in single compound sentences, as in the preceding exercise.

Complex Sentences   *TPS*, pp. 47–49

The compound sentence is easy to manage. You have only to link simple sentences together with one of the various connectives, most of which are in essence reducible to "and" or "but." The complex sentence, on the other hand, requires more thought; it requires you to examine the logical interrelationships between ideas, and to decide which idea is the more important. But let us be sure the definition is clear. A *complex sentence* **is really nothing more than a simple sentence (or** *main clause*) **delayed and elaborated with subordinate thoughts expressed in** *subordinate clauses*. **Whereas the** *compound sentence* **joins two roughly equivalent members by a coordinator, the** *complex sentence* **joins two unequal clauses by a subordinator. Three kinds of subordinators may connect the clauses:**

1. **Relative pronouns:** *that, which, who.*
2. **Subordinating conjunctions:** *although, if, because.*
3. **Adverbs:** *after, until, when.*

Exercise 7: Complex Sentences

Below are pairs of sentences, some of them the same pairs you converted to compound sentences in the preceding exercise. This time, convert them into complex sentences. And, again, list alternate choices—this time, subordinators.*

1. He couldn't go on. He was just too tired.

   ____

2. The crime commission recommended a number of such programs. Federal funds have been made available for putting them into operation.

   ____

   ____

   ____

3. We can probably never perfect the process beyond its present state. We should still try.

   ____

   ____

* To the student: you may have worked the first five sentences as part of an exercise in *TPS*, pp. 58-59. If so, begin with sentence 6.

4. Most schools are just now starting courses in computers for freshmen. To evaluate those programs will take several years.

______

______

______

5. On small farms, labor was not specialized. On medium farms, labor was partially specialized. But large farms carefully divided their workers into teams of specialists.

______

______

______

______

6. Few recipients of Social Security benefits can actually live on that income alone. Most supplement their incomes with savings or by selling the possessions of a lifetime.

______

______

______

______

7. We desperately need more judges and more staff. Courts are as much as twenty-six months behind schedule, with little hope of catching up.

______

______

______

______

8. An early reduction in the prime interest rate is not likely. House buyers are, therefore, reluctantly taking out mortgages with interests as high as 8 percent.

9. Within the past three years, jobs open to recent graduates have steadily shrunk. As a result, students are increasingly challenging the curriculum to provide them marketable skills.

10. An independent candidate for President has little chance of becoming a serious contender. He cannot rely upon large-party machinery, and he has little money for advertising.

11. Two motorists were killed last night when their car hit a guard rail, overturned, and caught fire. Police were unable to determine the cause of the accident.

12. Plants can obtain the elements for photosynthesis from water in the soil and from carbon dioxide in the air. Nevertheless, they need many other elements.

-----

13. Federal control of prices could have encouraged a switch to lead-free gasolines. The government could have legislated against higher prices for gasoline without lead additives.

-----

14. You may be familiar with our facilities and resources already. If not, simply fill out the enclosed form and return it to us, and we will send you a free brochure.

-----

15. True scientific knowledge is no longer accessible to the majority of us. We wish it were, but it just isn't. It's too complicated for most of us.

Exercise 8: Complex Sentences

From your own writing, supply five pairs of sentences. Then, just as you did in Exercise 7, revise the pairs into complex sentences.

Modifiers *TPS*, pp. 49–52

As we have seen, learning to handle the sentence well is largely a matter of both economy and precision. Active verbs communicate meaning more precisely, and they save words from their passive counterparts. A complex sentence can combine two simple sentences to clarify their relationship in fewer words. So handling the sentence well is largely a matter of learning to trim out the excess, to replace three words with two, to compress two sentences into one. *Modifiers* can achieve the same precise economy—and with added grace.

Of course, all along, your subordinating *ifs* and *whens* have really been modifying—that is, limiting—the things you attach them to. But there is a smoother way. You put the clauses and phrases directly against the noun they modify instead of attaching them with subordinators. For example, take this sentence: *John, who is usually very punctual, surprised everybody by not showing up at all.* Now put the modifier directly against the noun: *John, usually very punctual, surprised everybody by not showing up at all.* The direct contact of the noun *(John)* and its modifier *(usually very punctual)* cuts out a needless pronoun *(who)* and a colorless verb *(is)* with no loss of meaning whatever. It tucks information neatly into the sentence with a minimum of grammatical fuss. Let's take a closer look at five economical modifications: appositives, relatives understood, adjectives-with-phrase, participles, and absolutes.

APPOSITIVES *TPS*, pp. 49–51

A word, a phrase, or a clause may be set directly against a noun so that it clearly modifies the noun with no grammatical splice *(who is . . . that . . . which . . .)*. This puts the phrase "in apposition"; the phrase itself is an "appositive." *Fred, who is my former roommate* becomes *Fred, my former roommate.* You simply strike out *who is.* You can switch to *My former roommate, Fred* if you wish. But the appositive must always touch its noun, or the game is lost.

Exercise 9: Appositives

Streamline the following sentences by using appositives wherever you can.

1. Mark Twain, a Westerner who was flamboyant, loud, and perhaps even vulgar, had a surprisingly conservative and straitlaced Eastern wife.

2. The driving public will probably not accept the all-electric car, which is often mentioned as the answer to pollution, because it will prove expensive and troublesome.

____

____

____

____

3. Herman Melville, who is best known as a writer of exciting adventure fiction, spent much of his life in the thoroughly humdrum job of customs inspector.

____

____

____

____

4. The committee, which is composed of Dr. Gray, Dr. Phillips, and Dr. Alving, will conduct the oral examination.

____

____

____

5. One of the books on the list is *Art and Life in America*. As you know, this book won a Pulitzer Prize.

____

____

____

6. Waldo Adams, who is an expert on urban planning, denounced the idea as "visionary."

____

____

____

____

7. The football stadium, which is considered to be the best in the world, was completed in 1976.

____

____

____

8. Our ideas concerning Mars have been revised radically by data from the Viking probes. These data are still to be evaluated for many years.

____

____

____

____

9. *Romeo and Juliet*, which has been Shakespeare's most popular play from his day to ours, will be staged in a modern setting.

____

____

____

10. The company commended Marcia Bentworth, who is a native of Grand Bend.

____

____

____

RELATIVES UNDERSTOOD   *TPS,* p. 50

Often, a relative pronoun and a verb connect a modifier to its noun: *The man WHO WAS following him.* **But neither the pronoun nor the verb is really necessary, and the verb—often some form of "to be"—drains energy from the sentence's real verb.** *The man* **following him** *SHOUTED.* **Thus you can economically drop both the pronoun and the verb, leaving them "understood."**

Exercise 10: Relatives Understood

Eliminate relatives and their accompanying verbs from the following sentences:

1. The freeze on wages and prices that was announced by the President shocked European investors.

____

____

____

2. *Pygmalion,* which had first been popular as a play, and which had later been rewritten as a popular musical comedy, was finally done as a movie.

____

____

____

____

3. Although Picasso executed the original design, he had nothing to do with erecting the sculpture which is now standing in front of the Hancock Building in Chicago.

____

____

____

4. The studded tire, which has long been popular for winter driving in some states, is now being outlawed in many states because of damage to roads.

5. Because of the recession, the renovation that we had all hoped for has been postponed.

6. Students who are now being admitted to the master's program will not have to pass the foreign language proficiency test that has always been required in the past.

7. Either the operator or the patient himself can control the compressed gas that is respirated by the patient.

8. The various physical and chemical changes that are occurring must take place in a watery medium, or the ions, enzymes, and organic materials are not able to move about the cell and to diffuse to areas where they are required for metabolism.

---

9. The pumps which are now available have a fixed speed of 3450 rpm.

---

10. Radar operators couldn't identify the object that was causing the blip on their screens.

ADJECTIVES-WITH-PHRASE   *TPS*, p. 50

Often, we split a noun and its modifiers into different clauses or even into different sentences. *There was the lake. It was smooth in the early morning air.* **By simply placing the adjectival phrase against the noun it modifies (with a comma between), we can eliminate the redundant pronoun and verb.** *There was the lake, smooth in the early morning air.* **This is a neat and elegant construction.**

Exercise 11: Adjectives-with-Phrase

In each of the following sentences, move the adjectival phrase next to the noun it modifies, separating the two with a comma.

1. The commission's final report will probably not be ready for Friday's meeting. After all, the report is over 300 pages long and has more than 70 charts.

---

2. The street in Lawrence was completely familiar to Andrews. It was firmly rooted in his memory even after three years in the Army.

____

____

____

3. The narrator in *Autobiography of an Ex-Colored Man* was so light-skinned that he could easily pass for white, and when he finally decided to give up his black identity, he found it easy to do. Still, the choice left him bitter and embarrassed.

____

____

____

____

____

4. The crystal was cracked all the way through and had to be replaced.

____

____

5. Faulkner was ambivalent in his feelings toward his native South. He loved the land and its people, but hated what men had done to each other and the land.

____

____

____

6. They enjoyed the lawn. It was intensely green in the twilight.

____

____

7. His ideas were wholly unpersuasive. They were trite. They were borrowed. They were limp from his own lack of conviction.

____

____

____

____

8. The rabbit crouched by the wall. It was motionless. It was frozen with fear.

____

____

9. Its wheels were missing. Its bumpers, grill, and chrome had been stripped. Its windshield and windows were all smashed and jagged. The car had been thoroughly vandalized.

____

____

____

____

____

10. The curriculum has lost most of its original purpose. Although it is rich in variety, it is poor in basic courses.

____

____

____

PARTICIPLES   *TPS,* pp. 50–51

You can often weld a series of sentences together into one, graceful and smooth, with participles—verbs functioning as adjectives. Take, for example, this series: *George started to leave class. Then he changed his mind. And he quietly slid into a seat near the back of the room.* **Here are three separate verbs:** *started,* *changed,* **and** *slid.* **By turning two of them into present participles (-*ing* ending), and thus effectively making them adjectives, we can neatly fuse three sentences into one:** *Starting to leave class, then changing his mind, George quietly slid into a seat near the back of the room.* **We have saved three words, and gained some grace.**

Remember, the participle will make sense only when near its noun, with no other noun readily available. So don't walk off and leave the participle hanging with no noun to modify, or, worse, hooked to the wrong noun. The results of such *dangling participles* **are sometimes unintentionally funny:** *Perfumed, elaborately made-up, and elegantly dressed in a low-cut gown, the doorman was overwhelmed by the play's leading lady.*

Exercise 12: Participles

Keeping an eye out for dangling participles, revise the following sentences by transforming as many verbs as reasonably possible into participles.

1. After 100 miles, Hunt showed his winning style. He came out of each turn at 4000 rpm, accelerated to 8000 rpm on the following straight, then braked and shifted down for the next turn.

   ____

   ____

   ____

   ____

2. NASA doctors were worried about bacteria brought back from the moon by the Apollo 11 crew; consequently, they quarantined the crew for three weeks.

   ____

   ____

   ____

   ____

3. Mehevi saluted the old gentleman. Then he motioned him to sit down between us, and uncovered my swollen leg.

4. Nineteenth-century women were isolated and unenfranchised; they were sexually "used" and relegated to the kitchen and the nursery; in essence, society regarded them as brainless decorations.

5. He didn't check the charts for the water's depth and consequently ran aground thirty minutes after the race started.

6. The *Under Ground* eventually forced the mayor's resignation. It had seen a good opening for its running attack on the establishment. It had spread the lurid details over its pages week after week. It had alerted even the most conservative elements.

7. The assembly line was invented by Ford. It was institutionalized by the UAW. It is now extensively automated. It produces many components which are untouched by human hands.

____

____

____

____

8. Maureen started for the library. Then she decided to change her sweater. She spent the rest of the morning washing her hair.

____

____

____

9. It depends on the smoothness and porosity of the surface. It will also vary with the kind of wood. You should test the color of this stain on a small inconspicuous area and then thin it to the shade you desire.

____

____

____

____

10. Hemingway's life is intertwined with his work. Sometimes he reports almost straight autobiography as if it were fiction. Sometimes he transmutes autobiography into a new fictional reality.

____

____

____

____

ABSOLUTES   *TPS,* pp. 51–52

The absolute phrase is ordinarily nothing but a prepositional phrase with the preposition dropped. For example, take that last sentence. Drop the *with,* **add a comma to separate the phrase from the noun it modifies and you have:** *The absolute phrase is ordinarily nothing but a prepositional phrase, the preposition dropped.* **Or take a regular subordinate clause:** *Since the strike was resolved.* **. . . Now cut out the subordinator** (*since*) **and the finite verb** (*was*) **and you have,** *The strike resolved,* **. . . A noun and a participle. That is an absolute phrase, in this case an ablative absolute. Remember, the absolute must butt against the noun it modifies.**

Exercise 13: Absolutes

Try turning prepositional phrases and subordinate clauses in the following sentences into absolutes.

1. He got to the airport with less than twenty minutes to spare.

   ____

   ____

2. With mud splattered all over her stockings, she looked as if she had been out playing in puddles.

   ____

   ____

3. When the reviews were published, the producers decided to close the play.

   ____

   ____

4. Because Congress is not convened, extension of the draft is impossible at present.

   ____

   ____

5. Ted left the room when his examination was finished.

6. When September has arrived, the campus again fills with students, whose suntans glow and whose eyes sparkle with expectation.

7. Though it had been watered faithfully and had been transplanted in good potting soil, the plant died, with its leaves withered and curled and dropping on the rug.

8. Having gained a wide margin and leaving all challengers far behind, Adams easily won.

9. Because its planning had been faulty and its contractors were careless, the house was a continuous problem.

10. With the compound becoming a hazard to humans, the agency banned it from production.

Parallel Construction   *TPS*, pp. 52–56

Equivalent thoughts demand equivalent, or parallel, grammatical constructions. But writing is full of pauses and false starts. Scratching your head, or stopping for a cup of coffee, you rest between sentences. Or, interrupted by your roommate, you pause between clauses. You forget the present participles of an hour ago and slip into the past. Here is a checklist for your final draft (in the sample sentences, corrections are in parentheses):

> **1. Repeat connectives.**
>
> *By weeks of careful planning, by intelligence, by thorough training, and by a great deal of luck. . . .*
>
> *He prayed that they would leave and (that) the telephone would not ring.*
>
> **2. Match pairs: check terms on both sides of coordinating conjunctions.**
>
> *She liked the lawn and gardening (the lawn and the garden).*
>
> **3. Use paralleling connectors:** *both/and, either/or, not only/but also, first/ second/third, as well as,* **again matching pairs, noun for noun, adjective for adjective, participle for participle, and so forth.**
>
> *He is either an absolute piker or foolish (a fool).*

Exercise 14: Parallel Construction

Correct the faulty parallelism in the following sentences and clean up any wordiness you find. All of them, by the way, come from students' papers.

1. Twain seems eventually to become completely cynical, seemed to doubt even that any human life could be happy.

   ____

   ____

   ____

2. The Hemingway hero is a man who moves from one affair to another, who seeks adventure, enjoys bullfights, did a great deal of drinking, who was involved in activities we all wish we could try at least once.

   ____

   ____

   ____

---

3. Two of the factors to be considered in evaluating movie camera work are the placing of the cameras and the filters used.

---

4. Eddie Carbone is completely masculine, but Rodolpho has a girlish quality about him.

---

5. The playwright, Edward Albee, intended this play to be a comedy with a tragic ending. He intends us to laugh first and then to cry; however, appearing on stage last night there was very little comedy.

---

6. As a matter of fact, the Lantenengo Country Club claimed a long list of debauchery. For instance, Bobby Hermann, Whit Hoffman, and Froggie Ogden had caused a great deal of damage when, as a test, they lit some alcohol and caused an explosion. Ed Klitch had wandered up from the locker room stark naked and "ready for action." The musical instruments of a dance band had been totally destroyed by Whit Hoffman and Carter Davis. Kittie Hoffman won her purple heart by having her head stuck in the punch bowl by Carter Davis, after which she promptly returned the award with a kick to Carter's groin.

---

7. The only light coming from machine-gun fire and explosions, the audience is sure something exciting is happening, but what it is can't be seen.

8. In 1965, blacks numbered only 14 out of 863 students at Bronx High School of Science, 23 out of 629 students at Stuyvesant High School, 45 out of 368 at the High School of Music and Art, and out of 907 at Brooklyn Technical School, you could find only 22.

---

9. Near the end of Chapter 3, I get the feeling the situation is about to change when the narrator says of Caroline: "It was the time she did not fail him." The impression is given that the time is coming when she will fail him.

---

10. Either the sportscasters attacked the coach for poor recruiting, or he was criticized for his incapability in drilling the team.

---

11. By driving carefully, by making sure the engine was tuned, keeping the tires carefully filled, we were able to increase the gas mileage by about 18 percent.

---

12. We have seen that Wright was always fascinated by violence, that he had often seen violence first-hand, and he was himself a potentially violent person.

____

____

____

____

13. Not only did he delight in youth, but he had an almost pathological fear of growing old.

____

____

14. Either the report is incomplete or deliberately lying.

____

____

15. I remember seeing a pair of headlights coming at me in my lane, and a glimpse of the dense trees that lined the road on both sides. After that, nothing.

____

____

____

____

The Long and Short of It   *TPS*, pp. 56–57

Thus far, we have been talking about sentences as individual entities, each to be contemplated, revised, and polished. Now we shall consider the total stylistic effect of sentences working all together, the play of the short against the long, the intricate against the simple that makes a piece of writing move. Therefore, you must

revise your separate sentences with an eye for the total context, and an ear for the rhythm of your prose.

What do you look for? In essence, variety. You do not want sentences all of one pattern, however neat, nor all of one length. Either is monotonous. So try for the long and elaborate sentence, and try for the short. Mix in an occasional fragment. In a word, try for variety; experiment.

Exercise 15: The Long and Short of It

Below is an awkward and monotonous passage. One after another, the sentences march along—subject, verb, object—for nearly the same number of words. Rewrite the passage, giving its sentences variety in both pattern and length.

In 1911, Cal Rodgers was the first American pilot to attempt a successful coast-to-coast flight across the United States. He was tempted by the $50,000 prize offered by the Hearst papers to the first man to fly coast-to-coast in under 30 days. But as it turned out, poor Rodgers had to endure a lot of trouble and hardship and still did not win any of the prize money. First, he had to pay all of his own expenses for the trip, and that included the very high cost of having a train follow his route with spare parts. Admittedly, he was able to sell some advertising space on the side of his plane to a beer manufacturer, but he still finished the trip deeply in debt. Next, he had to travel an especially long and zigzag route because his tiny plane was not powerful enough to fly directly over the mountains. And to top it off, he had to put up with long delays for repairs both to his plane and to himself. He had 68 stops and 19 crashes and incurred a broken ankle as well as numerous cuts and bruises. When he arrived in California the plane he was flying was almost entirely different from the plane he had started with. In all, the trip took him 49 days and Rodgers covered the 3,390 miles distance in 82 hours of flying. His average speed was 40 miles per hour and his longest hop was 133 miles. And in the end, the Hearst papers did not award him the prize because he was 19 days over the stipulated time.

Correcting Wordy Sentences   *TPS*, pp. 61–68

Good sentences will ultimately come from constantly correcting the bad—usually wordy or ungrammatical, or both. And don't be discouraged if it takes time. As we write, we all waste words, take our thoughts as they come, and lazily accept the cliché rather than find a clear, fresh way of expressing an idea. The result, sadly, is a wordy draft, limp with passive verbs, filled with *the use of's and the fact that's,* weighted down with nouns, and flat with repeated patterns. Working out these bugs takes care, and practice. So learn to count words, to erase passive verbs, to subordinate, to tune the periodic sentence, and to follow the long with the short. Learn to be critical.

Exercise 16: Correcting Wordy Sentences

Below, you will find a series of first-draft sentences, some of them frankly ungrammatical, but most of them only mildly inept. See what you can do for them.

1. Summer is the time that more engines overheat than any other.

   ____

   ____

2. Your reluctance to supervise the project because of your lack of experience is quite understandable.

   ____

   ____

   ____

3. Both control lines are terminated in the console control section of Field 2 of the logic patch-board as shown in Figure 7.

   ____

   ____

   ____

4. The seminar will concern itself with a survey of government expenditure and revenue issues and is designed for students who wish to take a single comprehensive course in the field of public finance.

   ____

5. Each applicant is expected to apply simultaneously to extramural agencies and note these in his application to the Graduate School.

6. This is a book on social status in America that has the benefit of sure insight into the revolutionary changes that have taken place in the political and economic structure since the New Deal.

7. I was able to utilize much of your response in the text of my report and I deeply appreciate your taking the time to answer the questions so fully.

8. The major premise for the recruitment effort was to make personal contact between high school students and undergraduates a must.

9. Looking at the chart above, the significant results that I would like to call attention to are the poor correlation between the Congressman's perception of his constituents' attitudes and the actual attitudes of the majority of the constituents.

10. Either you must dial the full seven-digit number, or the two-letter prefix and five digits.

11. The dial tone is a low-pitched sound and it is continuous until the first digit or letter of the number you are calling is dialed.

12. Individuals whose income is insufficient to lift them above poverty must be provided with assistance from public sources.

____

____

____

13. In our company you will find wide-open opportunities for professional growth with a company that enjoys an enviable record for stability in the dynamic atmosphere of aerospace technology.

____

____

____

____

____

14. In the next thirty-five years it is expected that there will be more engineering work to be done than has been done in all of recorded history.

____

____

____

15. By cross-graining the veneer, the natural tendency of wood to shrink, swell, and warp is neutralized.

____

____

____

16. The federal government in Washington has recognized the need for regional planning of waste-water treatment, and has encouraged such planning through monetary incentives.

____

____

____

17. If expansion is not accomplished then two less efficient alternatives must be acted upon: either the book sales will have to be in separate quarters or else the whole enterprise will have to be moved to a larger location.

18. This article was written before the recent controversy concerning the relationship between the students working at the bookstore and the new manager, Fred Herlick.

19. Trees on average sites are expected to be about twenty inches in diameter when they are eighty years old if they are managed properly since youth.

20. On October 10, 1949, an unusually severe windstorm struck Wisconsin and the western half of the Upper Peninsula of Michigan. It caused heavy damage to forests by uprooting, breaking, splitting, or tipping trees.

21. I awoke at midnight, my bones aching and my back felt as if it were being pricked with electric needles.

22. My roommate is 6'8" in height, and he plays guard on the freshman basketball team.

23. Many debaters attack only the minor arguments of an opponent's speech which is never very sufficient or convincing.

24. Grazing peacefully like cattle, we saw a large herd of buffalo on the other side of the valley.

25. By putting the level in the horizontal plane and then looking through it, vertical distances from this plane can be measured.

26. The majority of railroad accidents involve people trespassing on rights-of-way or by automobiles running into the sides of trains.

27. Man, because of his numbers, now has the capacity to intervene massively in nature; i.e., to bring about major changes in the atmosphere, geosphere, hydrosphere, and biosphere.

28. Many factories are now being designed with an eye to attractiveness.

29. An ohmmeter is a direct reading device to obtain magnitude of resistance with low accuracy.

30. The errors made by employees are usually pointed out omitting the good work done.

____

____

31. The primary costs are for labor, transportation, and electric power.

____

____

32. I was standing by the window and looking into the street and two cars suddenly crashed together, and I ran outdoors to see whether or not anyone was hurt.

____

____

____

____

33. At least one day's notice is necessary to reserve a room for such a meeting.

____

____

34. Any amended declaration should be filed with the Internal Revenue Office with whom the original declaration was filed even if you move to another district.

____

____

____

____

35. Hospitalization for nearly every imaginable sickness or accident is covered by this policy except hospitalization caused by mental and nervous disorders or when confined in a Veterans Administration hospital.

36. Overall, automobile sales more than tripled from 1919 to 1929, in 1919 a total of 6,771,000 autos had been sold and by 1929 there were 23,121,000 passenger cars being driven.

37. Nowhere could I find any solid evidence that this actually happened.

38. Either we've got to cut back on electric power consumption or we've got to increase electric power production.

39. In 1956 the legislature passed a Soil Bank Plan whereby a farmer is paid not to harvest his crops but rather to put part of his land into cover crops.

---

40. It is expected that the new schedule will be announced by the bus company on Monday morning.

---

5 Words

Abstract and Concrete Words *TPS*, pp. 73–74

A good writer is always able to make his reader see and feel what he is talking about; he deals with clear and distinct images, with precise ideas. On the other hand, the poor writer, though he may himself have distinct images in mind, fails to put them across on the printed page because he does not bother to find the concrete, precise words for the job. He takes the easy way out, and chooses the abstract word. He somehow assumes that because the image is clear to *him*, it will be clear to his reader. But without the precise words, the image will stay only in his head. The reader will see nothing but mist.

Exercise 1: Abstract and Concrete Words

Revise the following sentences to make them more vivid and distinct by replacing as many of the abstract terms as possible with concrete terms.

1. Unhappy because of their lack of recognition, the Wright brothers quit flying in October, 1905.

   ____

   ____

   ____

2. For the better part of the year, he was without gainful employment.

   ____

   ____

3. Of the students who go to college outside their own state, 70 percent do not go back after completing their studies.

---

4. A sizable proportion of those people who use long-distance movers are large corporation employees whose moving expenses are entirely underwritten by their companies.

---

5. His great-grandfather once ran successfully for high public office, but he never served because his opponent mortally wounded him in a gunfight.

---

6. There was a severe disturbance in Jackson prison one day in the spring of 1952.

---

7. Convicts, armed with makeshift weapons, took some of the prison personnel hostage.

---

8. Her husband had one extramarital relationship after another and finally disappeared with a hotel dining room employee in one of our larger midwestern cities.

9. The lava issued slowly from the openings in the ground along the side of the trail.

10. Rejected by the military because of an impairment of his vision, Ernest became a journalist with a midwestern newspaper.

11. Hemingway was gravely injured when a trench mortar shell exploded directly behind him.

12. Several prominent labor leaders were entertained at the White House today.

13. Disadvantaged people are often maltreated by the very social-service agencies ostensibly designed to help them.

____

____

____

14. The newspaper reported that a small foreign car had overturned on the expressway just north of town.

____

____

____

15. The new contract offers almost no change in the fringe-benefit package.

____

____

Metaphor   _TPS_, pp. 74–77

In _TPS_, we considered four levels of metaphorical language. They are simile, plain metaphor, implied metaphor, and dead metaphor (see _TPS_, pp. 75–77).

All four levels, obviously, illustrate ideas by representing them in terms of their likenesses to physical things. All four paint pictures by which we can see abstract concepts. Thus, metaphor is particularly useful in conveying the writer's abstract perceptions to a reader by likening them to things the reader already knows. But metaphors often go wild. Blind to the specific implications of his images, one student wrote: "Large companies leave no stone unturned in their efforts to land their share of the economic pie." There the companies are, out in boats and equipped with fishing gear, turning over rocks, searching for pieces of pie! So, the trick is not just to create visual images, but to create those that work together.

Exercise 2: Metaphor

The following sentences, culled from students' papers, contain a number of metaphors, many of them abortive. About each metaphor, write a sentence or two of analysis and

evaluation. What is the image evoked? Is the image clear, fresh, appropriate? In short, does the image work?

1. Usually before the end of their third year, new junior executives in advertising companies pull up stakes and move on.
2. The year was 1935. America was caught in the grips of a nightmare she called the Great Depression.
3. The murmurs of the convention rose to the podium, cracking the facade of his imperturbability.
4. Richard was ecstatic with his success. He had scaled the mountain and from here on out he could sail with the breeze.
5. Whatever virtues the book may have, it has its faults too. For one thing, there are bogs of repetition all through it.
6. It is a sad reflection, but even the most well-meaning of governments is necessarily made up of men and, therefore, inevitably mirrors the faults and weaknesses of those men.
7. We have to be genuinely careful that concern for the environment does not become the hula hoop of the 1970's.
8. The advisor, obviously bored and tired after counseling a hall full of freshmen, spoke to me with all the enthusiasm and vigor of the telephone company's time-lady.
9. The prosecuting attorney leaned forward across the table toward the witness, resting his weight on one hand. He looked like an offensive lineman ready to lunge.
10. The letter was wilted, creased, and falling apart from being handled, like a road map that has been folded and unfolded so many times it just disintegrates.

Exercise 3: Metaphor

List five metaphors or similes from your own papers. After each, comment on the clarity, freshness, and appropriateness of the images.

Diction   *TPS*, pp. 78–82

Picking up a pen sometimes has a strange effect, like stage fright. Our language is rich with short, concrete Anglo-Saxon words and long, abstract Latin words, full of humor and wit, pleasant sounds and ugly sounds. Yet, somehow, the pen, like the stage, scares all that richness away. We are ordinarily full of humor; yet we suddenly turn grandly sober. We are ordinarily warm and personable; yet we suddenly grow distant and impersonal. In conversation, we are ordinarily vivid in our imagery; yet when writing we quickly slip into the dull, gray language of the committee. Up on the speaker's platform or down on paper, we use language as we never would anywhere else. For example, can you imagine yourself speaking this line?

> Partisan mutual adjustment is a decision-making process in which: a multiplicity of persons, representing decision-making influences, participate; no decision maker has an absolute authority over another, thus all agreements must evolve from a mutual concurrence of partisans; disjointed incrementalism is a feature of all decisions in the process itself; and the majority rule and the principle of equality are not strictly adhered to.

Speak it? Never. Write it? Alas, the answer is yes. This passage comes word for word from a college senior's paper.

But, because your language is rich, fully able to be at once clear, dignified, witty, and graceful, you need not settle for dull and wordy poverty. *Use* the language you have. Whether writing, speaking, or simply chatting with friends, make your words count. Aim for clarity first, economy next, then grace, and finally dignity.

Exercise 4: Diction

Here are some wordy, awkward, and flat passages from students' papers, with their wordage indicated in parentheses. In the space provided, rewrite each passage and indicate your own wordage. Make it less, and grow rich with economy.

1. Machines are merely amplifiers of the abilities of workmen, and exist only as they can do man's bidding effectively. (19)

____

____

____

____

2. Clearly, the only way to deal with machines is to neither flee from them nor surrender to them, but to use them as means to ends appointed not by them but by ourselves. (33)

____

____

____

____

3. The question is pertinent today, and painfully practical, as people examine the premises of their personal morality. (17)

____

____

____

4. Civil disobedience, then, is not the product of a recalcitrant minority intent on abolishing law and order, but exists in consequence of and as an important integral part of the give-and-take in democratic adjustment. It serves as a kick in the pants for legislators and the unconcerned majority, making them aware of faults in the democratic system. (59)

____

____

____

____

____

____

____

5. The criticism of the military in connection with the draft needs not be of only its character, which overshadows the draft machinery, but also of its direct involvement with the selective service system. The draft, an institution

created by Congress with the intention that it might be civilian-operated, administered by civilians for civilians, has become what it is today through the gradual infusion of the military. (67)

6. The ability to rapidly handle enormous amounts of data and make rapid decisions often enables the computer to do control applications, such as the generation of power at an electrical power plant. (32)

7. It is wrong to assume, although many criticisms are being raised against technology as it affects human values, that the author does not appreciate its great capacity for good. (29)

____

____

____

____

8. The candidate's record is completely in opposition to the aims of the United Auto Workers. (15)

____

____

____

9. As the establishment filled with people, an air of stuffiness and a feeling of being uncomfortable permeated the room. (19)

____

____

____

10. This reviewer, after reading about a dozen reviews of the book, was struck by the lack of perception and open-mindedness that the critics showed. (24)

____

____

____

____

11. With all the loud activity in the next apartment, the thinness of the walls became painfully apparent, and sleeping became impossible. (21)

____

____

____

12. The most essential prerequisite that any student group must have in order to be recognized as a power is a leader that acts both as a mouthpiece of the students' ideas and as an originator of students' strategy in their war against the administrators. (44)

13. When a student becomes a member of the Student Government Council, it is expected that he give up much of his spare time for the council. However, it is not, or at least should not, be expected that he quit school to take on the responsibility of a council member. (50)

14. Another fact which is revealed by the census statistics is that 72.4 percent of the total nonwhite population live in urban areas. (22)

15. A minority finds it difficult to progress in such a society due to the fact that a majority can perpetuate inequality by simply insuring that the vast majority of its members acquire the positions that pay the greater amounts of money and carry the greatest authority. (46)

16. It is not really any act which Julian commits which turns all his friends against him, but the fact that his sins are exposed publicly that makes him unforgiveable. (29)

17. Julian, a sensitive, kind, and honorable man, displayed, during his daily life, a courteous, well-mannered behavior obtained through good breeding, the only exceptions being when he was thoroughly intoxicated. (30)

18. Here, as the book leaves the war behind, it is finally apparent that Heller's comedy is his artistic response to his vision of evil; it is as though he is using laughter as an escape route from a malignant world. (40)

19. Through analysis of innumerable family histories, extensive tables have been compounded to give empiric risk factors for different heredity conditions. (20)

20. A major part of the task of maintaining or restoring a quality environment must be assumed by local governments in cooperation with, and with the support of, business interests, private organizations, and private citizens. (34)

21. The first thing that must be done is to define the problem. A concise analysis of the problem facing the environment is necessary if you are to fully understand the problem, formulate some specific action plans, and communicate your ideas to others. (42)

---

22. Continuous spending on the part of those with high incomes will have the eventual result of increasing prices, which further decreases the buying power of the poor man. (28)

---

23. There are two major results of the increasing mechanization of industry. One is a great reduction in the number of simple, repetitive jobs where all you need is your five senses and an untrained mind. The other result is a great increase in the number of jobs involved in designing, engineering, programming, and administering these automatic production systems. (58)

---

24. In the public schools, track systems, which attempt to put students of equal ability in the same types of courses, permit only a small fraction of high school students to take the type of courses necessary to gain admittance to college. (41)

25. But it can be observed in American business that often a curious cross between innovations to win customers and planned obsolescence to retain them became manufacturing policy. (27)

6 Research: Outlining and Documenting

Outlining for the Larger Paper   *TPS*, pp. 93–95, 105

The mind naturally categorizes and arranges ideas, grouping like with like. When you consider buying a car, for example, you immediately bring to mind two lists: advantages and disadvantages. When you answer a question in a quiz, you quickly visualize a list of points you want to make (assuming, of course, you have kept up with your assignments). And, as you have seen in the first five chapters of *TPS*, a simple scheme, such as *pro-con*, with a thesis statement will pull you through virtually all shorter papers. But for the more extensive research paper, a larger, more detailed outline is, more often than not, indispensible. With a little practice, you will find outlining helpful and time-saving in planning your large paper, and you will find that outlining also helps your inspiration along.

In the exercises that follow, we will examine three types of outlines: jotted, topic, and sentence. The sort of outline you write should depend only upon the length and complexity of the paper you are planning. However, let us first look at several principles basic to any form of outline.

1. Always begin the outline with a clearly labeled statement of your thesis, such as: "Thesis: Despite certain hazy benefits, we must admit that cigarettes are bad for us." Do *not*—as students sometimes do—enter the thesis statement as one of the major headings. (I. Despite certain hazy benefits, we must admit that cigarettes are bad for us.) Remember, start with a labeled statement of thesis.

2. As you plan your outline, rough it out first by working on only one level at a time. Work on the first level, or major headings, first. These are designated by Roman numerals. Then, when you are satisfied you have that under control, try the second level, the capital letters. And then the third level, the Arabic numerals. And so on. Trying to juggle more than one level of an outline at a time gets impossibly complicated.

3. Remember to arrange your major headings in the usual sequence of ascending interest and importance.

4. After you have roughed out the outline, check to see if you have any unpaired headings, that is, an A without a B, or a 1 without a 2. If you have, you are probably including an illustration or a detail too small for separate treatment. Go back and try to absorb or eliminate any such unpaired headings.

5. Now you are getting close to the end, but once again check your outline to make sure that your points will amply support and develop your thesis. Now is the time to spot and plug any holes in the logic.

6. As the last thing, check to make sure the headings of your outline are grammatically parallel and precisely stated. Grammatical parallelism reflects logical parallelism, and a failure to state your headings in grammatically parallel form now may break down the logical parallelism in your paper later. So go through the outline one level at a time and make sure the sentences on that level are all grammatically parallel.

The Jotted Outline

Jotted outlines are exactly what the name implies: a quickly jotted series of headings by which you plan to support your thesis. Often (but not always) developed on only one level, this outline is very much like the hasty sort of notes you might make for a simple speech—or the notes you would assemble on cards for a research paper (*TPS*, pp. 91, 93, 106, 108). You state your thesis, and under it list the four or five major ideas you want to be sure to bring in—single headings like "Loss of limb," amplified by phrases as necessary. Here is an example:

THE WICKED CIGARETTE

THESIS: Despite certain hazy benefits, we must admit that cigarettes are bad for us.

1. Social benefits—put you "in," give you something to do and say, make you feel mature (in charge of your own life).

2. Economic benefits—support a tremendous industrial network, from farmer to company to advertising agency to magazines and newspapers, providing thousands of livelihoods.

3. But moral hazards—become a habit controlling you, defeating your personal autonomy, making you "follow the pack."

4. Physical hazards—pose an unnecessary risk to the only heart and lungs you have.

Exercise 1: The Jotted Outline

Read the following essay and then make a jotted outline that describes the essay's structure. Use your own words to paraphrase the author's central idea and to state his supportive ideas. Do not simply quote sentences from the essay.

HOW A PRINCE SHOULD CONDUCT HIMSELF
IN ORDER TO ACQUIRE PRESTIGE

Nothing brings a prince into greater respect than the undertaking of great enterprises and setting a glorious example. In our day we have Ferdinand of Aragon, the present King of Spain. He may almost be called a new prince for, from being a very weak king, he has risen in fame and glory to be the leading monarch in Christendom. If his actions be studied, they will all be found great and some of them really extraordinary. Shortly after ascending to the throne, he attacked Granada, and that undertaking was the foundation of his state. For first of all he carried on the siege at his leisure and without fear of interference, and he kept the attention of the barons of Castille fixed on this war and thus unlikely to consider changes in the state, so that, almost without their being aware of it, he acquired great prestige and authority over them. The money from the Church and from the people enabled him to pay the troops and, in the course of that long war, to lay the foundations for his own army, which has since won so much honor for him. Furthermore, in order to prepare for greater enterprises, and always making use of the pretext of religion, he adopted the piously cruel policy of driving the Moors from his kingdom and despoiling them; herein his conduct could not have been more admirable and extraordinary. Still with the same pretext he attacked Africa, made the campaign in Italy, and has recently turned on the French. Thus he has continually been weaving some great design, which has arrested and amazed the minds of his subjects and kept them absorbed in the development of his plans. His projects have arisen naturally one out of the other and thus have afforded no time for men to pause and organize against him.

A prince should also give a good example in the matter of internal government, as in the case of Messer Bernabò of Milan, rewarding or punishing, as the occasion arises, the citizens who do good or evil in the service of the state, but taking care that the rewards or punishments be such as to cause comment. Above all a prince should see to it that his every action may add to his fame of greatness or excellence.

A prince is also esteemed when he shows himself a true friend or a true enemy, that is, when, without reservation, he takes his stand with one side or the other. This is always wiser than trying to be neutral, for if two powerful neighbors of yours fall out they are either of such sort that the victor may give you reason to fear him or they are not. In either case it will be better for you to take sides and wage an honest war. In the first case, if you do not show your sympathies, you will be an easy prey for the winner to the delight and satisfaction of the loser, and you will have no reason to expect anyone to defend you or give you refuge. For the winner will not care for unreliable friends who may abandon him in adversity, and the loser will not welcome you since you were not willing to take up arms and share the hazards of his fortune.

When Antiochus, invited by the Aetolians, had passed over into Greece to drive out the Romans, he sent a spokesman to the Achaeans, who were the allies of the Romans, urging them to keep out of the war. The Romans on their part were urging the Achaeans to join them. The situation was discussed before the Council of the Achaeans, and when the legate of Antiochus attempted to persuade them to remain neutral, the Roman envoy replied: "As to the statement that it is best and most profitable to your state to take no part in our war, nothing is further from the truth, for if you do not come into it you will be the prize of the victors without any prestige left to you and with no hope of consideration." And it will always fall out that a party unfriendly to you will ask you to remain neutral and those who are friendly will ask you to join them in the war. Irresolute princes, in order to avoid present dangers, usually follow the path of neutrality and more often than not are ruined. But if the prince chooses his side boldly, and his ally wins, even though the latter be powerful and the prince at his mercy, nonetheless there is a bond of obligation and friendship, and mankind is never so faithless as to show ingratitude under such circumstances by turning on friends. Besides, victories are never so complete that the victor need have no caution or respect for justice. But if your ally be the loser then he will welcome you and, as long as he can, he will give you aid and thus you will have a companion in your illl fortune which may yet rise again.

As for the second case, when the two contestants are of such stature that you will have nothing to fear from the victor, it is even more prudent to take part in the war for you will accomplish the ruin of one with the aid of the other who, had he been wise, should rather have supported him. For with your aid he is sure to win and, winning, to put himself in your power. And here it may be noted that a prince should never ally himself with one more powerful to attack another unless absolutely driven by necessity, as in the abovementioned cases. For if your powerful ally wins, you are at his mercy, and princes should avoid as much as possible being at the mercy of another. The Venetians joined France against the Duke of Milan when they could well have dispensed with their ally, and from this alliance came their ruin. Yet there are times when there is no help for it, as in the case of the Florentines when the Pope and the Spanish sent their armies to attack Lombardy, and then a prince must join one of the parties for the reasons set forth in the preceding paragraphs.

Let no state think that it can always adopt a safe course; rather should it be understood that all choices involve risks, for the order of things is such that one never escapes one danger without incurring another; prudence lies in weighing the disadvantages of each choice and taking the least bad as good.

A prince too must always show himself a lover of value and quick to honor those who excel in the various arts. Furthermore, he should encourage his citizens and enable them to go about their affairs in tranquility whether in commerce, agriculture, or any other kind of activity, so that one man may not refrain from improving his possessions for fear lest they be taken from him, nor another hesitate to engage in commerce for fear of taxes. Rather should a prince reward such citizens and any others who may in any way enrich his state or his city. He should also, on the appropriate occasions, offer festivals and spectacles for the diversion of his people, and, since every city is divided into guilds or clans, he should be mindful of these groups and occasionally mingle with them, giving an example of his humanity and munificence, always preserving, however, the majesty of his dignity, for this should never be allowed to suffer in any way.*

* Niccolo Machiavelli, *The Prince,* translated and edited by Thomas G. Bergin (Arlington Heights, Ill.: AHM Publishing Corporation, 1947), pp. 65-68. Copyright © 1947 by AHM Publishing Corporation. Reprinted by permission of the publisher.

The Topic Outline

The topic outline is an arranging of your jotted thoughts into more formal heads and subheads, each rank in parallel phrasing. Here you will notice two opposite currents: an inductive, uphill one, which carries your major heading toward your conclusion, and a deductive, downhill one, which partitions each major heading into smaller components. Here is an example:

THE PERNICIOUS VEGETABLE

THESIS: Although cigarettes have brought certain benefits to man, we must ultimately judge them harmful.
 I. Beneficial effects
    A. Benefits to society
       1. Income for the tobacco industry
          a. Farmers
          b. Wholesalers
          c. Retailers
       2. Income for the communications industry
          a. Advertising agencies
          b. Advertising media
       3. Income for the government
          a. National tax revenues
          b. State and local tax revenues
    B. Benefits to the individual
       1. Feeling of social ease and acceptance
       2. Feeling of self-responsibility
       3. Feeling of maturity
 II. But: harmful effects
    A. Income for criminal elements
       1. Vending-machine racketeers
       2. Narcotics and gambling racketeers

    B. Physical harm to the individual
       1. Historical opinions
          a. James I's condemnation of tobacco
          b. Thackeray's characterization of the cigar
          c. Edison's refusal to hire smokers
       2. Modern findings
          a. Impairment of physical stamina
             (1) Views of athletes and coaches
             (2) Personal experience in sports
          b. Relation to heart disease
          c. Relation to cancer
             (1) Laboratory findings: animals
             (2) Laboratory findings: humans
                (a) Lip cancer
                (b) Laryngeal cancer
                (c) Lung cancer
  C. Moral harm to the individual
     1. Surrender of one's individuality to the group
     2. Surrender of one's destiny to the habit

Exercise 2: The Topic Outline

Read the following essay and then develop a topic outline for it. Use the previous illustration as a model for your outline.

COUNTERFEIT MONEY

How to Detect Counterfeit Bills.—Years of experience have proved to the secret service that the best detector of counterfeit money is the properly trained human eye. The person who is best able to see the difference between the bogus bill and one that is genuine must know just what a genuine bill looks like. The only way such knowledge can be gained is through a careful examination of all parts of a genuine bill, and it is such a study that is advocated by the secret service to help Americans defend themselves against the counterfeiter.

The portion most difficult of good reproduction is the portrait on the face of every note. The portraits of famous Americans on United States paper money identify the denominations of the bills on which they appear, as follows:

$1	Washington	$100	Franklin
$2	Jefferson	$500	McKinley
$5	Lincoln	$1,000	Cleveland
$10	Hamilton	$5,000	Madison
$20	Jackson	$10,000	Chase
$50	Grant		

The genuine portraits are lifelike and distinct, and the shading which characterizes the facial features consists of numerous delicately executed dots and dashes. The oval background surrounding each portrait comprises a series of tiny squares, formed by the crossing of very fine vertical and horizontal lines. On most counterfeits the portraits are defective in the shading in the face, and many of the little squares in the background are filled with ink or are flecked with white where the vertical and horizontal lines are broken. In the genuine portrait the eyes are always clear and expressive, but in most counterfeits they are dull, distorted or otherwise executed so that they do not compare favorably with the genuine.

These differences alone between the genuine and counterfeit portraits prompt the secret service advice to the individual to compare any questionable bill with another of the same type known to be genuine. Such a comparison will make evident any differences between the two to such an extent that if one is counterfeit it can be classified as such.

Only three types of currency are in circulation in the United States—(1) federal reserve notes; (2) United States notes; and (3) silver certificates. The latter two are no longer issued. Part of the design of every genuine bill includes the treasury seal, a small circle edged with sharp points like the teeth of a saw, enclosing an angle square under which is a key and over which is a balance scale, all mounted upon a dotted white shield within the circle. Surrounding the design are the Latin words *Thesaur. Amer. Septent. Sigil.*, representing the "Seal of the Treasury of North America." On silver certificates the seal and the serial numbers are printed in blue; on United States notes they are in red, and on federal reserve notes, in green. Thus, the type of any bill may be quickly determined merely by the color of the treasury seal and the serial numbers. In addition, the words "Silver Certificate," "United States Note" or "Federal Reserve Note," as the case may be, are engraved at the top center of the face of a bill.

On many counterfeits the sharp points around the outer edge of the treasury seal are blunt or broken. Here again, a comparison of the seal on a questionable bill with the seal on a genuine bill will show the difference.

The serial numbers of genuine United States paper money are printed in a distinctive type style, and numbering blocks of the kind used for this purpose cannot be obtained except by the bureau of engraving and printing. Therefore, in producing a counterfeit, the counterfeiter must either use numbers unlike the genuine, or must try to copy the genuine numerals. In the first instance a comparison will show the difference in the style, and in the second instance the copies or imitated numbers are usually poorly spaced or crookedly aligned, so that a comparison will indicate they are not authentic.

The border design of every genuine bill includes an intricate lacelike network of fine white lines. The patterns for these lines are produced by a machine known as a geometric lathe, and the lines are technically called geometric lathework. In a genuine bill these lines are clear and unbroken, but on most bogus notes the border is too dark because many of the spaces between the lines are filled with black ink caused by inferior etching, or perhaps too light because the white lines are thicker than the genuine, creating a bleached appearance. . . .

How to Detect Counterfeit Coins.—The manufacture of spurious coins does not involve losses as great as those suffered by victims of counterfeit bills. This is due, of course, to the fact that there is a wide margin of difference between the value of metal money and the representative value of paper money.

The passer of counterfeit coins depends upon the carelessness of his victims in the same way as does the passer of counterfeit bills. Genuine silver coins [and alloy coins issued today] have a corrugated outer edge, known as the reeding. Consisting of evenly spaced ridges, this feature was included on silver coins originally to prevent unscrupulous persons from cutting or filing from the edges of the coins small bits of silver, which they would then sell for the intrinsic value of the metal so derived. Later, however, the reeded edges of silver coins formed considerable protection against counterfeiting since the corrugations on most bogus coins are only partially executed, unevenly spaced or entirely missing in places. Thus, a comparison of a questionable coin with one known to be genuine, or even a careful scrutiny of the ridges around a questionable coin, will usually indicate whether it is good or bad.

Most counterfeit coins are made of metal alloy which does not ring as clearly as genuine coins when dropped on a hard surface and which is usually much softer than silver. Therefore, questionable coins should be dropped on a hard surface to test their ring and should be cut with a knife to test their quality. If a coin sounds dull or is easily cut, it is undoubtedly a counterfeit.

It is also a fact that most counterfeit coins feel greasy, so it is wise to feel all coins, and if one feels slippery or greasy it should be further examined for defects in the reeding or other characteristics.*

*Frank J. Wilson, in *Encyclopaedia Britannica*, 14th Edition (Chicago: Encyclopaedia Britannica, Inc., 1970), Vol. 6, p. 646. Reprinted by permission. © Encyclopaedia Britannica, Inc., 1970. This article has been slightly modified to bring it up to date.

The Sentence Outline

You will probably find that the jotted outline and the topic outline work best when you are doing expository papers or comparatively simple argumentative papers. The more argumentative your paper, however, the more likely you will find the sentence outline useful. Because every subdivision in the outline is presented in full sentence form, the completed outline will provide you, in skeletal form, with the whole substance of your argument. Thus the sentence outline should enable you to spot any defects in your logic and to gauge the effectiveness of your defense. Study the following outline.

CERVANTES

THESIS: Cervantes's chivalric idealism and realistic experience combined to produce his masterpiece, *Don Quixote,* which laughs at idealism only to endorse its realistic application.

  I. Cervantes's chivalric romanticism was natural to him.
     A. He grew up when romances were in vogue.
     B. His own family, though poor, was ancient and presumably noble.
     C. He read romances avidly.
     D. His first and last writings were serious attempts at idealistic romance.
 II. But, being poor, he led a harshly realistic and disappointing life.
     A. He experienced the hardships of a soldier abroad.
        1. As a private who saw service in several foreign campaigns, he was long stationed in Italy.
        2. He fought the Turks at Lepanto, suffering a wound that crippled his left hand.
        3. He was a captive of Algerian pirates for five years.
        4. Ransomed, he returned to Spain at the age of thirty-five to find neither recognition nor pay awaiting him.
     B. He turned to writing for his livelihood.
        1. He began with an idealistic romance, a kind of writing he continued throughout his life with little success.
        2. He tried the picaresque tale, the story of rogues and vagabonds.
III. From these two strains, the high and the low, came the idea for *Don Quixote*—a parodying of high chivalric romances through low situations.
 IV. Cervantes's genius made this simple contrast great: he created two great characters to represent the two sides of the contrast.

Exercise 3: The Sentence Outline

Using the outline shown above as a model, develop a sentence outline for the following essay on limiting the Presidency of the United States to a single term.

> *The Hon. Mike Mansfield*
> *United States Senator, Montana, Democrat*
> *Senate Majority Leader*
> *Testimony before the Senate Constitutional Amendments*
>   *Subcommittee,*
> *October 28, 1971.*

I welcome the chance to express my views pertaining to the proposed Constitutional Amendment that would limit the Presidency to a single term of six years. I am particularly proud and pleased to join with the distinguished Senator from Vermont* in this endeavor which I per-

* The Hon. George D. Aiken.

sonally regard as one of the most important reforms that our system of government could undergo.

In recent years there have been a number of significant amendments to the Constitution of the United States. Correcting the matter of Presidential succession and particularly extending the franchise of the ballot to young adults 18, 19 and 20 years of age represent enormous steps forward: steps that protect and enhance immensely the Democratic processes of this Nation. In my judgment there is still another step that must be taken in this area of Constitutional evolution. It is only in providing a single Presidential term of six years, I believe, that this Nation will preserve for its highest office a sufficient degree of freedom and independence to function properly and adequately today and in the years ahead; years that will produce enormous trials and tensions on the national and global scale, some of which have yet to emerge.

By no means do I intend to imply that with this proposed amendment new ground is being broken or that a topic of first impression is here being raised. Indeed, the suggestion of a single six-year term has been with us ever since the delegates to the Constitutional Convention of 1787 thrashed over the question of a President's term and his eligibility for re-election. It is interesting to note that popular election was not considered with any great favor at all during the proceedings of that convention. But proposals limiting the tenure of the Presidents were put forth and discussed. Ultimately none were approved and the question then became moot when the suggestion for an electoral college system gained the widest support.

Since the Constitution was ratified hundreds of amendments have been introduced in the Senate and House of Representatives proposing a change in Presidential tenure. More than 130 of these recommended a single term of six years. Twice, the House reported legislation providing for the six-year term. And in 1913, the Senate passed S.J. Res. 78 calling for a term of six years, but no action was taken by the other body. Presidents themselves have been most active in their support for the concept. Nearly 150 years ago Andrew Jackson recommended that the electoral college be abolished—also a good suggestion—that the President be elected by direct vote, and that he be limited to a single term of either four or six years. Presidents Hayes and Cleveland and William Howard Taft also offered the proposal. In more recent years on this issue I have followed the lead of the able and distinguished Senator from Vermont, the dean of the Republicans and a wise and prudent judge on all matters and particularly on those affecting the needs of democratic institutions in a rapidly changing world. That brings us up to today, and I must say that the merits of the proposal dictate its need now as never before.

It is just intolerable that a President of the United States—any President, whatever his party—is compelled to devote his time, energy and talents to what can be termed only as purely political tasks. I do not refer solely to a President's own re-election campaign. To be sure a re-election effort and all it entails are burdens enough. But a President facing re-election faces as well a host of demands that range from attending to the needs of political office holders, office seekers, financial backers and all the rest, to riding herd on the day-to-day developments within the pedestrian partisan arena. Surely this amendment does not represent a panacea for these ills which have grown up with our system of democracy. But it would go far, I think, in unsaddling the Presidency from many of these unnecessary political burdens that an incumbent bears.

Clearly such a change to a very great extent would free the President to devote a far greater measure of his time to the enormous task of serving all of the people of this Nation as Chief Executive. More time would thus be provided for policy-making and policy-implementing, for program initiating and for shaping and directing the kind of Administration a President chooses. More time would be provided for the kind of experimentation that a successful Presidency requires; such experimentation has come too infrequently in recent years, and as a Nation we suffer from that inadequacy. . . .

To sum it up, what this amendment seeks is to place the office of the Presidency in a position that transcends as much as possible partisan political considerations of whatever nature and source. That it cannot do the job completely, I would agree. The man who achieves the office carries with him his full political heritage. But its adoption would do much, I think, to streamline the Presidency in a manner that ultimately will make the position more fully responsive to the concerns of all Americans.*

*The Congressional Digest, March 1972, pp. 80-84.

Documenting Your Sources   TPS, pp. 95–103

In pursuing a line of exposition or argument, you should credit all ideas not your own. Good documentation is part of thorough, efficient research. As you have seen in TPS, most documentation begins with a quotation or summary in the text, and the details, which would clutter the prose of exposition or argument, fall into footnotes and bibliographies. Preparing footnotes (and bibliographies, which follow from footnotes) puts off most writers, but the two basic patterns are simple: author, title, city of publication, publisher, date, and page for books; author, title of article, name of periodical, date (or volume and number), and pages for magazines and newspapers. Your footnotes should suffice to lead your reader to the ideas you have borrowed if he wants to read them further. Review TPS for varieties of the basic patterns, then work the following exercises.

Exercise 4: Documenting Your Sources

1. **Assume that you are quoting the following passage in its entirety, and that you have not mentioned it, or its author, earlier in your paper. Devise a sentence to**

introduce the passage, quote the passage, and give it a footnote number, then write a footnote covering the necessary bibliographical data. The author is Gilbert K. Chesterton. The book, *Heretics*, was published in 1905 by John Lane, in London. The passage is on page thirty-eight:

> When Byron divided humanity into the bores and bored, he omitted to notice that the higher qualities exist entirely in the bores, the lower qualities in the bored, among whom he counted himself. The bore, by his starry enthusiasm, his solemn happiness, may, in some sense, have proved himself poetical. The bored has certainly proved himself prosaic.

2. **Now write a sentence referring to Chesterton's point that a bore may be poetical, quoting directly only the phrase** *his starry enthusiasm.* **Assume that you have already fully cited Chesterton, and give your reader whatever bibliographical information this new quotation demands.**

3. **Write four footnotes illustrating the four different kinds of sources, described below, for the same hypothetical fact:** *300 dropouts annually.*

   A. You found this in an article with these characteristics:

Quarterly magazine entitled:	Schools and Scholars
Volume number:	Forty-nine
Author:	Gladys P. Spencer
Page:	One hundred three
Date:	January 1976
Title:	Our Local Schools

   B. Write the same footnote as if the magazine were a popular weekly dated January 10, 1976.

   C. Write the same footnote to your statistic as if you had found it, together with a full citation of this article in the popular monthly, on page 460 of a book entitled *Education for Educators* **by Featherbush Brown, published in Philadelphia in 1980 by the P.J. Slacks Company, Incorporated.**

   D. Write the same footnote assuming that you found Spencer's statistic on page forty-nine in a collection of essays entitled *Readings for Reading,* **which Beatrice Long and Bernard Short edited, which the Grimm Publishing Company produced in 1980, in New York City, and which has reprinted Spencer's article.**

4. **W. L. Cranberry has written the following two studies, both of which you want to cite:**

   Book: The Dying Locomotive
   Article: Transportation No Problem

   First, write a footnote for the book—Verity and Company published it in Miami in 1981—in which you inform your reader that the author's full name is Walter Lightfoot Cranberry. You have quoted from page one.
   Next, assume that you have already given the first full citation for both the

book and the article. Now write footnotes 3 and 4, footnote 3 for the book, foot-note 4 for the article, providing page numbers.

5. Write a summarizing footnote, including the following phrases and abbreviations: *c., see, ed., see also, ch., ff., rev., et al., passim,* and dealing with the following supposed items:

   A. An essay entitled Too Many Cars by L. A. Crump, in an anthology called Traffic edited by Arlene Pringle and several others, which the Willing Company pub-lished in New York in 1978 and then revised in 1983—you wish to refer your reader to an extended account beginning on page ten.

   B. Certain statistics have become available only from about 1920.

   C. Wilma May Smithers, whom you have already cited in full, says something on her page four that the reader should compare with Crump; the reader should also look at her sixth chapter.

   D. Griffin, another writer you have already cited, takes a generally hostile view of Crump's work.

   E. You want the reader to consult also the entry about automobiles in the *Encyclopaedia Britannica,* volume dated 1987.

6. Make a bibliography, listing one entry each from exercises 1, 3, 4, and 5, adding hypothetical page numbers, if necessary.

7 Grammar and Mechanics

Grammar   *TPS*, pp. 122–135

Grammar and mechanics put your thoughts in shape. They also put you in shape before your audience. Each detail has meaning; each carries a message. The agreement of subject and verb, of pronoun, of modifier, makes your ideas clear. The differing pauses and stops of commas, semicolons, and periods signal differences of meaning, and keep your reader from stumbling in bewilderment. Accurate grammar and mechanics also tell your audience that you know what you are doing, that you are in control of yourself and your thinking, and that, consequently, what you are saying is worth attending to. This message is almost worth the whole game. No matter how worthy your thoughts, if you appear before the public with something unzipped, that public will tend to look down and write you off. To persuade, then, keep your prose and your speech zipped up and buttoned down. These exercises will help you to do so.

Exercise 1: Grammar

A. Treat these ailing sentences. In your cured versions, underline the simple subject of each clause once, and the subject's verb twice. Underline any other changes, and put brackets around subordinate clauses where you find them.

SIMPLE SENTENCES

1. The old and the young, the feeble and the sprightly, joins the dance.

2. John Stevenson liked everything about the old town, her relatives, and she most of all.

3. There is one or two things left to do.

4. Solving several specific problems are good exercise.

5. Ann, as well as her mother, like to sew.

COMPOUND SENTENCES

6. He drives the car, and she, a friendly girl, do the talking.

7. Jim drove the car, and her friends think him crazy.

8. They liked the dinner, but they forget to thank Gertrude and I.

9. Either the bed was too hard, or it is too expensive for one night.

COMPLEX SENTENCES

10. While leaving the stadium, the game was over.

11. Whenever he comes, a party could be expected to begin.

12. Them who gets there first gets the best seats.

13. After all these years, they still envied him succeeding in everything he tried.

14. The old and the young, the feeble and the sprightly, comes when the drum

begins to beat.

15. All the people, whoever happened to be in the village, was welcome.

B. Revise the following sentences, correcting the awkward shifts of subject, person, and number:

1. A stitch was dropped, and Barbara sighed.

2. Whenever a stitch was dropped, Barbara would sigh.

3. Sam sat down at the counter, catsup was poured on the hamburger, and

there was hunger in his face as he ate it.

4. These statistics are impressive, but error is evident in them.

5. The United Nations is not so firmly established that they can enforce inter-

national law.

6. One should never assume that they have no faults.

7. A person is overwhelmed by the gardens. Everywhere you look is beauty.

8. People distrust his glibness. One feels they are being taken in by him.

C. Treat these troubles, mostly verbal:

1. The committee were miles apart.

2. None of these proposals are unworkable.

3. Neither the question nor the answers seems pertinent to the issue.

4. John was the second one of the fifty boys who has volunteered.

5. Each who have come this far have shown real determination.

6. His idea of fine foods are hamburgers and French fries.

7. Last year we are warned of higher taxes and getting lower taxes. This year we are promised lower taxes and getting higher taxes. What next year is holding, we can only guess. But sooner or later we are being promised and taxed into disbelief.

D. On a separate sheet, straighten out the inconsistencies of tense, voice, and mood in this cripple:

> A third principle that industry should recognize was the need for constant appraisal by management of an employee's progress. Management would determine what a person, when he or she would of been hired, were expected by it to achieve; and it then judges whether it now had had that person poorly assigned. They probably know their own limitations, and jobs beyond their capacity are poorly handled by them. But it is not enough that a manager sit down periodically with employees and reviews their performance. The important thing is that the manager understands a person well enough and be articulate enough to make sure the person haas become conscious of needs for further development. If the manager will have been sufficiently observant, he might have helped his employees to an accurate evaluation of their own potential.

E. Cure the disabled pronouns:

1. They cheered both of us—Andy and I.

2. I admit it was me to whom they first confided.

3. We all three like it—Helen, Ann, and myself.

4. Us sophomores should all sign the petition.

5. Both her and me were elected.

6. He told her and I to leave.

7. They always elect whomever is popular.

8. They choose whoever they like.

9. Everybody thinks us girls should go.

10. Little love is lost between him and I.

11. In the end, it was them who succeeded.

12. The child who he adored finally broke his heart.

F. Rescue the dangling modifiers:

1. Surviving the blast, the emergency treatment revived him.

____

____

2. All cars without registration stickers parked in lot 3 will be towed away.

____

____

3. John gave Bill all his clubs, bag, and other golfing equipment.

____

____

4. When lifting the table, the chessmen slid off the board.

____

____

5. The hunters resumed shooting the game birds after they reloaded.

____

____

G. Strengthen the faulty references:

1. He sent him his high-school pictures.

2. He kicked the child's toy by accident who was visiting.

3. Everyone knows their own best interest.

4. He missed several classes, which in the end defeated him.

5. When industries fail to make plans far enough into the future decades, they often underestimate them.

6. She ended her performance, but it was too late.

7. He opened the bird's cage, and it flew away.

8. My family is always throwing their weight around.

9. Shakespeare has Edgar portray his essential position.

———————————————————————————

———————————————————————————

10. These sort of snakes are very deceptive in their coloring.

———————————————————————————

———————————————————————————

11. The roofers finished early, after last touches to the trim and shingles, and they had really made it sparkle.

———————————————————————————

———————————————————————————

———————————————————————————

———————————————————————————

12. She loves swimming especially in the surf, thinking it the best exercise in the world.

———————————————————————————

———————————————————————————

———————————————————————————

13. His article was accepted by *Sport* magazine, for which he acknowledged his gratitude.

———————————————————————————

———————————————————————————

———————————————————————————

14. People should insure themselves against death and accident. These provide for the welfare of their loved ones.

———————————————————————————

15. There is a sandwich shop by the police station, and we phone them when we get hungry.

16. Coaches sometimes ignore the best interests of their players for the sake of winning games, and they are angry if they lose them because of bad grades, after working them too hard.

17. When he had his last heart attack, it almost stopped beating.

18. A governor should know a little about law and a lot about people, and apply them diplomatically.

H. Cure the faulty modifiers:

1. Everyone feels badly about it.

2. She sang melancholy.

3. The bidding began quietly and leisurely.

4. The work of a student is more intense than his parents.

5. It was a near perfect shot.

6. Some girls have expectations beyond a husband.

7. Industry is as strong if not stronger than before the depression.

8. The workman did not feel well enough to continue.

I. Bring these sentences to full health:

1. The only light coming from machine-gun fire and explosions, it is hard for the audience to see whom is hit.

____

____

____

2. The audience, as well as the cast, were glad when they were finished.

____

____

3. If the Administration would have checked into the activities that were being done by the Democrats in an honest manner, they would have avoided the mess of Watergate.

____

____

____

____

4. Either the report is incomplete or deliberately lying to both the public and he personally.

5. Not only did he delight in youth, but he had an almost pathological fear that it was already too late to enjoy it.

6. They study hard here, but you do not have to work all the time.

7. The contest between Louise and I was decided by only the absentee ballots, and they totaled them inaccurately.

8. Walking to the game, it was decided to give the team their due, whether or not it was going to bring us the championship.

9. Speaking before the committee, everything he said damaged his case.

10. Every member of the committee had tried to keep their minds open.

11. He sat his briefcase carefully on the desk, hoping it would not be too late to use the evidence in it, and left it laying there when he answered the phone.

12. She was awakened by a loud knocking, which turned out to be across the hall where they were installing a new floor.

Punctuation   *TPS*, pp. 139–155

Again, the medium carries the message—indeed, a twofold message. Punctuation signals the meaning of your words, marking those differing pauses that make your meaning clear in speech. Punctuation also signals that you yourself know what you mean, that you are in control, that you know what's what. So brush up on the meanings of the various signals with these exercises.

THE PERIOD   *TPS*, pp. 139–140, 163–164

Briefly, periods go: (1) after a declarative sentence, (2) after an indirect question, (3) after a polite command or request, (4) with most abbreviations.

Exercise 2: The Period

Some of the following sentences have correct periods; some run together without punctuation; some fumble the period in various ways. Insert the proper punctuation in the faulty sentences.

1. I have only a faint recollection of the place of my childhood at times, I can close my eyes and call up vague images, but most of the time I just can't remember.

2. Norm got to the theater a little after 8:00 PM, but everyone had already gone.

3. Killens's short story deals with Joe, a soldier on his way to Korea.

4. Sitting down in front of the TV set, I kicked off my shoes and loosened my belt, still, I felt very nervous and tense.

5. You asked whether I planned to go to the party after the show, well, I certainly do.

6. Two of these packages are headed for Washington, DC, the third is going to Baltimore.

7. Please climb down you'll hurt yourself.

8. The COD order arrived just after lunch on Thursday afternoon, but since Jim didn't have any money, the driver wouldn't leave the package.

9. The International Brigades, which were formed by Comintern to fight in Spain, were a combination of displaced and dissatisfied people from all over the world, many of the first to join were people forced by Fascist governments to leave Germany and Italy.

10. During the Depression, Wright held a number of jobs he was a hospital orderly, a counselor in a boys club, a newspaper correspondent.

11. Go ahead help yourself to all the salad you want, there's going to be plenty to go around.

12. In studying the similarities in the courtroom strategies of Boris Max and Clarence Darrow, one can also find parallels between the characters themselves, their lives, their attitudes.

13. Thank you for your answers to my questionnaire I will be able to use much of your response in my report.

14. Applications for the freshman class are down 5 percent, but about 55 percent of the total applicants will still have to be turned away.

15. Sunday, May 23, at 4:00 PM, there will be a symposium on drug abuse. Interested students should contact Mr Leach at 764-1425.

16. He asked me how the goods would be distributed?

17. Attention please, pets are not to be brought into or through this building.

18. The law school has reached an all-time high in applications. With 13 applicants for each of its 370 openings.

19. About 1,000 scientists from 25 foreign countries are expected to attend the workshop. Where 180 papers will be presented.

20. WEB DuBois received his PhD from Harvard in 1895.

21. In order to gain a full understanding of any book. One ought to know something of the life and intellectual background of its author.

22. He argued that by 5 o'clock this evening we would know how many people to expect for the party I think he's wrong.

23. Shortly after 9 PM Mrs AK Moore was attacked from behind by a purse-snatcher.

24. People seldom form their own judgment about politics they let others form it for them.

25. Although the lawyer knew that his client was guilty. He defended him vigorously so that he could gain a reputation for victory, if not for justice.

26. I awoke at midnight, my bones were aching and my back felt as if it were being pricked with electric needles.

27. At first glance. This plan seems satisfactory, but it is an almost impossible task to make the selection it requires.

28. The first two costs omit gas-content of the metal whereas the third includes it.

29. Modern society is built on the automobile every child looks forward to the time when he can drive.

30. Like space, time is a natural organizer. Ancient. And simple.

THE COMMA   *TPS*, pp. 140–147

Put a comma: (1) before *and, but, for, or, nor, yet, still* **when joining independent clauses; (2) between all terms in a series, including the last two; (3) to set off parenthetical openers and afterthoughts; (4) before and after parenthetical insertions (use a pair of commas).**

Exercise 3: The Comma

Correct the following sentences, inserting commas where needed, removing them where not (and, in a few cases, inserting periods). As before, some of the sentences are correct as they stand.

1. This report will discuss the equipment to be used, the procedure to be followed the data to be obtained and the format for presenting the results.

2. We find however that the greatest expense in renovation will be for labor not for materials.

3. This book, even after seventy-five years, is still one of the finest examples of sociological scholarship available and it ought to be required reading in any elementary sociology course.

4. The French Revolution of 1789 sparked a similar revolution led by Toussaint L'Ouverture, in Haiti in 1791, and shortly thereafter the French recognized the freedom of the slaves.

5. Remote sensing devices exploit parts of the electromagnetic spectrum invisible to the eye.

6. The council appointed Professor Donald Sandburg, chairman of the Resource Allocation Commission, to be head of the new project on this campus.

7. Will Sexton a long-time member of the department will become sales manager on July 1 but until that time he will remain on convalescent leave.

8. Tight money and a scarcity of jobs have given a boost to graduate school applications.

9. He depended for his quotations upon the Bible Shakespeare and Emerson.

10. A faithful sincere friend he remained loyal to his roommate even after the unexpected disagreeable turn of events.

11. We were delayed by the heavy snow, and therefore did not arrive in time for the lecture.

12. Although few readers of *The Adventures of Huckleberry Finn* recognize it at first the book is really a somber story of treachery murder and brutality.

13. Robert E. Lee was born at Stratford Virginia on January 19 1807.

14. In America said the Chinese lecturer people sing "Home Sweet Home." In China they stay there.

15. Should the estimate be too high I will seek other bids.

16. Printed in London bound in New York and first released in Chicago the book cost so much its sales were very limited.

17. The jobs of these machine operators largely assembly-line workers have become as simple repetitive and mechanical as the functions of the machines themselves.

18. Readers of Joseph Heller's book *Catch-22* a comic novel about World War II seem to react in one of two ways. Either they love the book or they can't stand it, in either case the book seems to arouse their passions.

19. Depressed refusing to face the reality of his situation he killed himself, it was as simple as that.

20. Writing in a popular magazine the critic said that Rex Harrison as Henry Higgins and Wilfrid Hyde-White as Colonel Pickering stole the show.

21. Jill Crabtree, in her article, "Foreign Relations at Home" says that American students are not interested in the foreign students on this campus despite the campaign by the International Center to promote their interest.

22. I guess I could drive the truck myself, still I really don't want to.

23. Person-to-person calls collect calls credit-card calls and calls to be billed to another telephone must be placed through the operator.

24. Either Rob gets an extension on his lease or he will have to move out of his apartment before May 1.

25. With the advent of refrigeration both in the home and in conveyances, the housewife could feed her family fresh foods in any season, before that she had fresh foods available only in season, and her winter menus were nutritionally weak.

26. In "Indian Camp" Hemingway's short story the reader's attention is on Nick Adams an eight- or ten-year-old observer of the jackknife Caesarean that his father performs on the Indian woman. We watch the watcher so to speak.

27. Although there are areas of overlap this report is divided into five parts: General Activities Criteria The Committee's Influence Upon Classified Research Communications and Future Considerations.

Remember this basic premise: the semicolon ordinarily goes only where a period *might* go. (1) It is best as a kind of tight period to separate sentences closely related. (2) Before conjunctive adverbs (comma after), it also joins independent clauses: for example, *; however,* or *; therefore,* or *; moreover.* (3) Finally, it separates a list of elements containing internal commas.

Exercise 4: The Semicolon

The following sentences include examples of both correct and incorrect semicolons. Insert them where needed; remove them where not. Adjust commas and periods as necessary.

1. The book deals with the folly of war, its stupidity, its cruelty, however, in doing this the author brings in too many characters, repeats episodes over and over again, and spoils his comedy by pressing too hard.

2. Despite these shortcomings; however, the book has remained popular because it is fresh and wacky in its approach.

3. Most men smoked either cigars or pipes, for a long time cigarettes were regarded as unmanly.

4. Most men smokers used either cigars or pipes; most women smokers used cigarettes.

5. Steinbeck's fictional strike in *In Dubious Battle* is not unique, in the 1930's such strikes were very real indeed.

6. The endowment provides stipends for periods of from six months to a year. The scope of support includes: language, both modern and classical, literature, jurisprudence, philosophy, ancient, historical, and modern, archaeology, history (of Western Europe only) and sociology.

7. Your comments should be specific, pointed, and candid, you should not hold back anything.

8. We need to create a new kind of academic community, one with a spirit of openness; the student must be able to find meaning, coherence, and significance behind the jumble of experiences he gets.

9. Many graduating students are scared to death. The job market hasn't been so tight since the 1930's.

10. The law library will be open from 8 A.M. to 11 P.M., now through December 21; from 8 A.M. to 6 P.M., from December 24 to January 4, and closed Christmas Day and New Year's Day.

11. To let him go unpunished was unthinkable, to punish him, unbearable.

12. In McKay's novel, *Home to Harlem*, Jake's character remains rather constant, however, his friend Ray undergoes a fairly substantial change.

13. Although the story was written in 1933; it shows few of the characteristic marks of the period's popular literature.

14. On the one hand, it is obvious that Mr. Bisko disagrees with the company policy, on the other hand, if he wants to keep his job he has to put up with it.

15. Probably only 5 percent of the potential jobs for naval architects and marine engineers are actually held by people who are trained for them, in fact, probably 50 percent of these jobs are held by people who aren't college educated or technically trained at all.

16. When the Department of Defense needs something; it often needs it quickly and in enormous quantities.

17. The address selector is normally operated by the control panel pushbuttons, nevertheless, it can also be operated by a digital computer; or from the logic patch-board.

18. The following documents are enclosed with the agenda: minutes of the regular meeting of the Board of Directors of November 23; Annual Report on Financial Affairs; Annual Report of the Planning Committee.

19. A colon is a green light; a semicolon, a stop sign.

20. Sir Thomas Hobbes believed that there was an absolute order (not always apparent) operating in the external world, that is, he thought everything

that happened had a rational and logical cause.

21. Deists believed in a "clockmaker God" they believed He made the universe, set its wheels in motion, and then went off and left it.

22. For Bigger Thomas, Christianity was symbolized by a burning cross; for his mother, by a crucifix.

23. The tentative book list includes: *Last Exit to Brooklyn*, by Hubert Selby, *Dangling Man*, by Saul Bellow, and *1984*; by George Orwell.

24. The players were delighted, the managers, appalled.

25. The vegetables produced in an organic garden may be beautiful; however, there is nothing pretty about a compost heap!

26. Remember, when the semicolon is used sparingly; it retains its tight-lipped emphasis, used recklessly; it merely clutters your page.

THE COLON   *TPS*, pp. 147–148

Primarily, a colon introduces an itemized series, a formal quotation, a clarifying detail, or an illustrative example. Use a colon as a green light, or arrow.

Exercise 5: The Colon

In the following sentences, some colons are right, some wrong, some missing: correct all errors, including misused periods, commas, and semicolons.

1. The music is generally excellent; the tunes are quite good and the singing clear and bright.

2. Ralph Ellison, describing in *Shadow and Act* how he switched his interest from music to literature says; "Writing provided me a growing satisfaction and required, unlike music, no formal study. . . ."

3. There's only one thing we need right now—more time.

4. Remote sensing devices exploit the following parts of the electromagnetic spectrum; infrared radiation, ultraviolet radiation, gamma rays, and microwaves.

5. We're out here for one reason only, to work with Dr. Ravelli.

6. The semicolon, as we have seen, makes a full stop; the colon waves the traffic on through the intersection, "Go right ahead," it says, "and you will find what you are looking for."

7. For assistance call any of the following staff members, Mr. Beatty, 714-1425, Mr. Greenway, 714-2829, Mr. Brooks, 714-4432.

8. A project may be given a national security classification to provide project personnel access to classified information, to facilitate visiting classified activities, counseling, and participating in advisory functions: or for reasons related to the work statement.

9. There's one thing you can say: the plot is timely.

10. This attitude is caused by two things; first, students in a large university tend to think of themselves as being lost in the crowd: and, second, students tend to view administrators—as administrators sometimes view themselves—as substitute parents.

11. Of Faulkner's short stories I think the best is "Red Leaves:" my favorite of Faulkner's novels is "Absalom, Absalom!"

12. Yeats's "Collected Poems" which includes "Sailing to Byzantium" is always good reading: Joyce's short story collection, "Dubliners," is equally fine as reading.

Spelling   *TPS,* pp. 155–158, 180

Benjamin Franklin, who long advocated reform in spelling, once said something we probably all feel at one time or another: "As our alphabet now stands, the bad spelling, or what is called so, is generally the best. . . ." The fault, he thought, is not with the speller, but with the English system of spelling itself, with the alphabet. That may be consoling. For here we are, 200 years later, still waiting for reform and still stuck with enough eccentricities in English spelling to keep us all thumbing the dictionary, perpetually uneasy. Franklin notwithstanding, you will scarcely convince most readers that you are a reformer if you spell *alphabet, alfabet,* or *spelling, speling.* Actually, English spelling is a good deal more systematic than it seems. Here are some suggestions that might help:

1. We commonly misspell a great number of English words because we also commonly mispronounce them. For example, *February, existence, athletics, optimism, surprise, government, intramural, environment.* Check through the words you often misspell to see if you are also characteristically mispronouncing them. Watch especially for the words that tend to get slurred over. For example, students will sometimes carelessly write *could of* for *could have,* or *prejudice* for *prejudiced.* Pronounce it, and you will see why. In short, check your pronunciation. The fault may well be there. If so, correct the pronunciation and the spelling will correct itself.

2. We commonly misspell words because we forget about a few simple rules of English spelling and of the exceptions. For example, the familiar old rule:

> *I* before *e*
> Except after *c*
> Or when sounded like *a*
> As in *neighbor* and *weigh.*

Try it out on *receive, conceive, believe, achieve.* Or, as another example, the rule:

> Double the final single consonant before a suffix beginning with a vowel if the consonant is the last letter of a one-syllable word, or if it is the last letter of an accented syllable, and if it is preceded by a single vowel.

Try that rule on *stop (stopping), stoop (stooped), begin (beginning), rain (raining), remain (remaining).* That works too. Or the rule:

> Drop the final e before a suffix beginning with a vowel but not before a suffix beginning with a consonant.

For example, *caring, cared,* but *careful, careless.* In short, remember the old rules.

3. We commonly misspell a number of words in English because they are, frankly, tricky. With words like these, memory is almost the only answer: *loose, lose, personal, personnel, beneficial, category, controversial, embarrass, its, it's, their, there.* Keep a list of the words you routinely misspell. Memorize them.

Exercise 6: Spelling

To help you identify your likely errors, here are some sentences with a number of commonly misspelled words. Correct each misspelling you find, marking a line through it and writing the correct spelling above it. Then list the five words that give you the most trouble.

1. Marrage seems to be loosing some of it's traditional signifigance as the devorce rate continues to climb and common-law relationships multiply.

2. Writting is neccessary in almost any proffession.

3. Many woman feel there acheivements go unrecognized.

4. Offering an explaination is uneccessary unless the personal director asks for one.

5. Certainly one of the most contraversial issues to come along in years, abortion reform has sparked heated arguements in most churches.

6. The proffessor said he would reccomend at least 3 possable sources.

7. I value your opinion.

8. He had a good sence of rythm but a terrible ear for pitch.

9. The preformance last night was embarassing, a suprise considerring the ammount of rehersal time the actors had.

10. Environmental deterioration is probobly the single most disasterous consequence of overcrowding.

11. The wittness was able to supply a good discription.

12. Ammong the words on this page, your likely to find at least a few you commonly mispell.

13. There is really no point in studing the definations of words unless at the same time you make an effort to incorperate them into your speech.

14. Students who have transfered from other schools will recieve credit only for those courses in which their grades were above C.

15. The audiance wasn't conscience that anything unusual had occured, but during the third act the leading man broke his collar-bone when he was topled back over the couch in the fight scene.

16. The principle reason for the written examinition is that it allows us to spot canidates who's work isn't likely to meet company standards.

17. The city counsel studied each of the items on the agenda seperately and in it's proper sequence.

18. George gets embarrassed whenever anyone pays him a complement.

19. The committee voted to except the treasurer's annual report, but decided to delay any final judgement on the new buget till after all the members had time to anilize the implications of the previous year's figures.

20. The sucessful businessman usually combines aggressiveness with caution; he is willing to take risks but carefull to minimize those risks as much as possible.

21. There's no point in exagerating the significants of Saturday's loss.

22. Heros are often apologetic about their accomplishments.

23. The curriculum has changed remarkably during the passed 20 years.

24. He may be ingenius but he's certainly no genius.

25. To divide is to seperate.

26. One of the curious side-affects of long contact with DDT seems to be an increased resistance to cancer.

27. Primative versions of the television reciever had tiny screens, barely 4 inches accross.

28. Children often become irratable in the late afternoon.

29. The acknoledgements and the forward precede the table of contents.

30. The Secretery sited the current drop in interest rates as an encouraging sign.

Capitalization   *TPS*, pp. 159–160

Capitalization, and the italics that go with it in titles, is really a part of punctuation, signaling the difference in meaning between *truth* **and** *Truth,* **for instance. The con-**

vention of beginning each new sentence with a capital letter is probably as familiar to you as turning a door knob, and requires as little attention. But the other conventions are less familiar, and even experienced writers, constantly practicing their craft, must sometimes check the less frequent ones in a handbook. So look over the conventions in *The Practical Stylist* and see if you can restore the original capitals and italics in the following paragraphs.

Exercise 7: Capitalization

Add capitals and italics to the following paragraphs.

1. the oldest independent black people in the western hemisphere are the bushmen of surinam on the north coast of south america, the descendants of negro slaves who escaped from their dutch masters early in the 1600's, according to the greenhill star-advertiser. they set up strategically scattered villages, raided plantations for black women and supplies, and successfully fought all campaigns against them, even those conducted by experienced european commanders. aphra behn, in her novel oroonoko, or the royal slave (1688), especially in her preface, praises the handsomeness, intelligence, and bravery of the surinam negro. thomas southerne repeats the impression in oroonoke: a tragedy (1695), a play based on mrs. behn's book, especially in act i, scene iii. two u.s. blacks from harvard, s. allen counter, jr., a neurobiologist, and david l. evans, admissions officer, have studied the bush people for five years and have produced a documentary film entitled the bush afro-americans of surinam and french guiana: the connecting link. "these people," says counter, "represent to american blacks a mirror of the best example of what we would have been like had we chosen not to live in slavery and had removed ourselves to another place."

2. religious wars are the worst, as we can see in both the near east and the british isles, specifically in lebanon and northern ireland. the german motto gott mit uns ("god is with us") of world war i becomes an attitude

excluding the other side from all justification and humanity. it generates fanatical dedication and hatred, as a recent article in the new republic suggests. when moslem fights christian, and catholic fights protestant, each sees his side as right with a religious fervor, as unlike his enemy as day and night, yet all are identical in their fanaticism unto death, like the ancient zealots, in their unquenchable dedication to revenge and ultimate victory for the cause even in the distant future. dr. roger shinn, reinhold niebuhr professor of social ethics at union theological seminary, new york city, points out that war and religion both ask dedication beyond self. when the two combine, the dedication doubles, and all compromise seems evil, a betrayal of truth, and faith, and the right way.

77 78 79 80 7 6 5 4 3 2